QUESTAR PUBLISHERS, INC.
Sisters, Oregon

What woman doesn't need help in determining her priorities? About the time she feels comfortable with the order of her life — WHAMMO! — another change comes along forcing her to reexamine her priorities.

It was during one of these times that Cheryl Biehl appeared in my life to give me the help I needed. Her personal experience, wisdom, and example can help any woman to make her life more significant.

VONETTE BRIGHT
Campus Crusade for Christ

I was at a point in my life where I felt everything was out of control — the demands of a household, an infant, a two-year-old, and a husband were overwhelming to me. After going through Cheryl's study I realized there were countless things I could accomplish if I just took the time to figure out my priorities and goals, actually write them down, and then work step by step, day by day, to see those goals become realities.

ANNETTE NEWCOMB

God has given me only a certain amount of time on this earth. I want to use that time as best I can — keeping my priorities straight. In an interesting and easy-to-follow manner, the material in this book is helping me in that endeavor.

CHRIS STANFIELD

for when you feel like screaming...

I Can't Do Everything!

The Christian Woman's Guide to Focused Living

CHERYL BIEHL

I CAN'T DO EVERYTHING
© 1990 by Cheryl Biehl

Published by Questar Publishers, Inc.

International Standard Book Number: 0-945564-29-5

Printed in the United States of America

TO BOBBY

THE MAN I MOST ADMIRE

A SPECIAL THANKS

. . . to my imaginative daughter, Kimberly Anne,
who formulated the title,

. . . to the three focus groups who gave me
invaluable feedback as I wrote this book:

Carolee Winrich
Karen Masters
Robin Webster
Annette Newman
Lisa Schwanner
Delia Pyle
Chris Hrisca
Kay Lou King
Debbie Meumann
Chris Gencarella
Shelly Sander
Kim Carpenter
Debbie Gilbert
Ellen Sambrano
Karen Stoney
Cindy Munson
Anne Bunce
Sally Hales

and,

. . . to my very dear friend, Anne Lehman,
who spent many hours editing the manuscript.

CONTENTS

INTRODUCTION

Your

North Star

"I LOVE YOU," Bobb said as he squeezed my hand. "You're a great travel agent."

American Airlines Flight 29 had carried us to an altitude of seven miles above the icy Atlantic. We were with my parents, returning home from Europe. We were celebrating our anniversaries: their 50th and our 25th.

Our gift to my parents had been this trip to some of our favorite spots on a favorite continent. Warm tears moistened my eyes as memories which would last a lifetime flooded my mind: a cruise down the Rhine; the Matterhorn, gold-tinged at sunrise; a magical Mozart concert in a fortress overlooking Salzburg; a horse-drawn carriage tour through the quaint streets of Vienna; and countless hours of conversation while traveling the fabulous Eurail train system. Most important was the almost three weeks spent together in celebration of two outstanding marriages and relationships between family friends. Everything for which I had hoped and planned in the preceding months had, in fact, taken place.

During the long hours of the plane ride home, I began a quarterly "to do" list — things I needed to complete within the next two to three months. There were 43 things on that list. I don't mean simple things, like feeding the dog; I mean major projects, like finishing the writing of this book. I knew I had to donate the first week back home to jet-lag recovery and the second to catching up in my office. Realistically, I knew I couldn't begin the work of chiseling away at the list for two weeks after my return.

My warm sentiments about the trip began to turn to depression and feelings of being overwhelmed as the reality of the work I needed to do in the near future enveloped me.

I remember turning to Bobb and expressing my thoughts. I remarked how I wished someone had already written this book so I would know where to begin. His response was encouraging: "Cheryl, I've watched you pull yourself out of similar circumstances a thousand times before. Just take notes on how you do it, and you'll have your book."

I took my husband's advice — and you'll find meat on those skeletal bones on the pages that follow.

First, I went before God and focused on who I am and who He is. From that perspective, I asked what is most important for me to do. I reevaluated and revised my list by extending some deadlines and eliminating a few others. I filled my quarterly, weekly and daily calendars with those carefully chosen remaining priorities.

Now, after two and a half months, I look back and smile — not only because I completed my list, but also because I liked the choices I made. I did the things that were most important to me.

How do you cope with all that life demands of you as a Christian woman in today's overextended world? Do you find yourself juggling the many hats of household taxi driver, travel agent, correspondent, nurse, tutor, coach, encyclopedia, psychologist, nutritionist, referee, and answering machine?

You've been told that every woman today needs to fulfill her personal ambitions, so you further your education, do aerobics, and join a therapy group.

Then, as a Christian, you're expected to participate in church activities, so you attend a weekly Bible study, volunteer to make crafts to sell at the annual bazaar, and teach a Sunday school class.

Does this schedule sound familiar? Do you feel pulled in a hundred directions by things which all seem to be legitimate priorities? Do you ever feel like screaming,

"I CAN'T DO EVERYTHING!"

On the office door of our church's youth pastor hangs a sign which reads, "Don't 'SHOULD' on Me!" A friend recently expressed a similar feeling by saying the word *should* should be eliminated from our vocabulary.

God set down some absolutes that He commands us to obey. But the point of the youth pastor's sign is well taken. Apart from necessary governmental laws and a very few other exceptions, no one has much right to impose his "shoulds" on you.

With that in mind, let me assure you that I will not attempt to tell you what you *should* do.

However, this book is written for Christian women, and the absolutes that God clearly states in His Word will be discussed here as indisputable values and courses of action which must be followed. You will find the golden thread of spiritual values woven within the tapestry of this book. If you are not a Christian, my prayer is that you will discover how deep, wide, long and high is the incredible love of God for you.

If you follow the steps as outlined, they will show you how to sort out what is most important for *you* as a Christian woman. As you pass through different seasons in your life and are introduced to new options, your priorities will change, paving the way for new goals.

The first chapter of this book encourages you to draw near to God and find out who you are in relationship to who He is. When that is clearly established, you can move on to sorting out priorities for yourself — for your lifetime, for this particular season of your life, for this year, this quarter, this week, and for today.

THIS IS NOT a book to sit down and read like a novel, nor is it a true workbook. It's more of an instruction manual to help you get in touch with who you are as a child of God, and with what you most want to do. There are no absolute right or wrong ways to organize your life. If you don't like my methods, use your own. Create a customized system which meets your personal needs.

Whatever else this book does, I hope it makes you think. I hope it challenges you to make every minute effective, whether you are working, playing, or resting. Each of us has the same sixty seconds in each minute, the same sixty minutes in an hour, the same twenty-four hours in a day, the same seven days in a week, the same fifty-two weeks in a year. And only God knows how many years we have. Time has a way of slipping by; Monday turns into Tuesday, Tuesday is suddenly Wednesday — and at end of the week you may not be sure what you've accomplished.

If you establish your priorities ahead of time, you will most likely do what you determined to do. In deference to what's *best*, you'll be able to say no to what's merely *good* without feeling guilty.

The fundamental principle of this book is simple: Go before God to decide what to do with your life that will please Him; then break your goals down into manageable units and carry them out...one step at a time.

At this point, I'd like to give you a little warning: Working through this book will take time. Planning takes time, but lack of planning takes more time in the long run. Taking one hour now may save you ten hours or even a hundred hours in the future. I encourage you to invest the time required to set up systems that will in effect multiply the hours in your lifetime.

You may find it helpful to work through this book with a friend or group of friends. Such an interaction with others not only can stimulate thought but also may eliminate the temptation to put off completing suggested exercises. Such procrastination can rob you of any realized benefits. If you work through this manual with other people, your good intentions are likely to be converted into action.

You'll find discussion questions at the end of each chapter. These can be used by a group or pondered by you as you work independently.

Many recommendations in this book have already helped many women just like you. But only you can transform those recommendations into a plan and a system that becomes your North Star to follow. Customize the system to fit your individual needs.

Don't let this book overwhelm you. *Work through it.* I strongly suggest that on each page you complete the exercises as proposed before proceeding further. In this way you build upon a foundation step by step.

Different people will require different amounts of time to complete the book and to put into operation the system that best maximizes their daily living. If you're tempted to think you don't have time to set up such a system, remember that the busier you are, the more you need it.

At the end of each day, week, and year — and at the close of your life — I want you to look back and be able to say, *"I like the choices I made for the time I was given. I did what I actually wanted to do, and what I believe pleased God."*

DISCUSSION QUESTIONS:

1. Make a "to do" list of what you need to do in the next ninety days. Do you feel overwhelmed? If so, is this a long-term or temporary situation?

2. Look back on the last ninety days. Do you like the choices you made? Are you satisfied with your choices, or do you feel that you "wasted time"?

3. Do you find yourself setting all your goals because of what other people say you "should" do? Does this conflict with what you *want* to do?

4. Are you willing to take the time and effort necessary to determine what is best for you to do with the rest of your life?

1

Focusing

Your

Heart

✧

My STOMACH WAS IN KNOTS. I sat in my living-room chair, tears flowing down my cheeks. I was burdened for a close friend who was in a very dangerous situation. Little else could penetrate my thoughts.

"Honey, when was the last time you ate?" asked my mother on the phone.

"I don't remember... I think I had a cracker yesterday about noon." Eating hadn't occurred to me. I was totally overwhelmed by my friend's situation.

Then I remembered the Old Testament prophet Elisha's prayer to open the eyes of his servant. Do you remember the story? It's found in 2 Kings 6. Elisha was an old, blind prophet, but he had "eyes" to see what his young servant couldn't. Elisha apprised the Israelite king of war plans being made by the enemy, the king of Aram. After losing a string of battles, the king of Aram thought there was treason among his troops. But upon thorough investigation, he discovered that Elisha was the informant.

So Aram's king sent soldiers to destroy the old man. When Elisha's servant looked out and saw an army with horses and chariots surrounding the city, he assumed the odds against Elisha and himself were overwhelming. He informed the prophet that they were in serious trouble.

I love Elisha's reply: "Don't be afraid. Those who are with us are more than those who are with them." I can picture the servant smiling over Elisha's obvious blindness. And then Elisha prayed: "O Lord, open his eyes so he may see." Miraculously, God allowed the servant to see what He already had shown Elisha: "hills full of horses and chariots of fire all around."

Remembering the story, *my heart relaxed.* I realized that this same Sovereign God had sent His angels to surround my friend, even as He had Elisha. Who was I to worry? I continued the vigil of prayer, but I knew God was in command. How arrogant and presumptuous of me to think my anxiety could do something that God's angels couldn't. God had commanded me to leave my burdens with Him; yet I had continued to worry.

When my heart turned and became focused on God, I was able to release my worry about my friend's situation to His sovereign control, and my burden was lightened. Don't misunderstand; I did not put a giggle in my voice and forget the situation. Rather, I concentrated on how big God is. I knew now He certainly could handle my friend's problem. And He did — news soon came that my friend was out of danger and unharmed.

But what if the news had been that my friend actually was harmed, or even killed? Would this have indicated that God had turned His back on me or my friend? NO! God *always* works according to His own purposes. In Romans 8:28-29 we are promised that all things WORK (it does not say all things *happen* for good, but that God takes those circumstances and *works* them for good) together for the good of believers, in order to conform us to His image. He sees our lives from an eternal perspective, without time or other limiting factors. It's like the difference in perception between looking down on a big city from an airplane, versus looking up from a sidewalk surrounded by skyscrapers.

You may never understand why God allowed something to happen, but it's at this point that you must put your trust in the One who sees the world from the comprehensive aerial view. *Confidence in His sovereignty may be the only assurance you ever have in this life.* As you stand on the sidewalk of life, the skyscrapers around you may block your vision of God's purpose. But in eternity those skyscrapers come tumbling down, and all things will be clearly understood. Paul tells us that today we see through a glass darkly, but someday, when we stand face to face with Jesus, our vision will be as through crystal-clear glass.

AS A CHRISTIAN, the most critical consideration in getting your life in balance is to focus your thoughts and the desires of your heart.

To *focus your heart* means establishing an understanding of who God is, who you are, and where you fit in the broad scope of eternity — for this year... this month... this week... today. Since I also struggle to maintain this delicate balance, I'd like to share with you some of the habits I've established which help me keep my heart and mind focused on Jesus.

As you read about these habits, you may determine that at this time in your life, you simply cannot include all of them. If this is true of you, I urge you at least to take time to focus your heart on God and who He is. When your situation changes, you may decide to add another dimension to your time with God.

SETTING TIME ASIDE DAILY

The God of the Bible doesn't assign points in His cosmic gradebook for numbers of hours spent in prayer, numbers of buckets of tears produced while praying for a friend's health or salvation, or how much hurtful persecution is experienced as a result of "sharing your faith."

I am not suggesting that you rush to God each morning to have Him put a check mark by your name for some righteous ritual you've completed. I *am* suggesting, however, that you come to Him in prayer each morning to draw close to Him... to focus on Him... to receive your focus for the day.

I prefer coming before God each morning so that I can reflect on my time with God throughout the day. Perhaps you're a "night person." You may prefer evening time with God so you can "sleep on it" and think about it the next day as well. Choose the time of least distractions for you.

Spending time with God *does* take time. It *is* a commitment. Let me emphasize again, however, that the spiritual exercises described are not "shoulds" intended to inflict guilt if you are not able or don't care to execute them. They are simply options from which you may choose those which suit your personality and particular needs at this time in your life.

I remember well the first time I was challenged to get out of bed fifteen minutes earlier than usual to make time to pray. My friend Lynda and I set our alarms for 6 A.M. We committed to pray, upon hearing our own alarm, that the other person would get out of bed and begin her day with a time of prayer. Later that day we talked by telephone, giving an account to one another of whether we had overcome the temptation to sleep longer. It seemed to be the crutch we needed; soon we both were surprised when the extra fifteen minutes we budgeted was not enough to complete our prayer time.

That was the beginning for me. It still isn't easy. My bed still entreats me to linger there each morning, but years of experience convince me each morning that I want to get up more than I want to sleep. For me, nothing can exceed the joy of spending time at the feet of our Lord.

IMAGINE YOURSELF COMING BEFORE THE HOLY GOD OF HEAVEN

God commands us in the Bible, "Be still and know that I am God." Take the time right now to picture yourself approaching the throne of Almighty God. What do you see? Think about His Deity and your humanity... His Holiness and your sinfulness. Worship and praise Him, for He is God Almighty. Always come before Him in prayer with an attitude of worship and praise.

It is imperative that you confess your known sins before you make requests of God. In Isaiah 59:1 we read a solemn warning:

> Surely the arm of the Lord
>   is not too short to save,
>   nor His ear too dull to hear.
> But your iniquities have separated
>   you from your God;
> your sins have hidden his face from you,
>   so that he will not hear.

Surely there can be no sin worth risking separation from your God, with the result that your prayers go unheard. If unconfessed sin is in your life, I urge you to confess it. Open that line of communication with your Heavenly Father.

I am convinced that it is virtually impossible for a Christian to draw near to God's throne with unconfessed sin in her life. At least it is for me. Either I avoid His nearness (if I'm unwilling to confess that sin) or I confess it. But I cannot hold a cherished, unconfessed sin and stand before Him. Confession is a major step in focusing my heart.

Continue this exercise of standing before Almighty God. (You may find it meaningful to take notes to refresh your memory of this time for the future.) You're standing before the Eternal Throne, all known sin confessed. As you stand there, be acutely aware of who you are. You are a human being, absolutely unworthy to stand before God the Father on your own merit. But He chose you to be His child for all eternity. He made this possible through His Son, Jesus Christ. Not only has He forgiven your sin, but He has transferred Jesus' righteousness to you.

You are His child. He cares about you even more than we as human mothers know how to care for and love our own children. He cares about your problems, your hurts, your victories and your defeats. He invites you to spend time in His presence because He loves you.

My response to this is, "Why me, Lord? Why

did You choose me to be Your child?" I am
eternally grateful. Love overwhelms my heart as I
fall to my knees before Him. I am ready to
worship Him. I am ready to listen to Him. I am
ready to give Him complete control of my life.

All that I am — my assets... my strengths... my
liabilities... my fears... anxieties... hurts... past
sins... reputation — all of these I leave with Him.

All that I have — Everything we have comes
from God. He can take it away at any moment.
Today, how does He want to use what He has
given me for His glory?

All that I hope to be — my dreams...
fantasies... goals... He is free to eliminate or
change any of them. Or He may choose to
expand them to greater heights than I have ever
dreamed.

READING FROM GOD'S WORD

The next step in focusing my heart is to read from
God's Word. I like to begin by reading a portion
in the Old Testament. It affords me an historical
perspective and gives me insights into things that
please God but which are not commanded in the
New Testament.

As I read the Old Testament, I am amazed at how slow to learn God's people seem to have been. I am highly critical as I see them repeat the same cycle of failure without seeming to learn any lesson at all: They sinned (their usual sin was building idols in "high places"), God placed judgment on them, they repented, and God forgave. But before long they would sin again in the same way, and the cycle would repeat itself.

Then I look at my own life. With great distress I realize that I am equally guilty. The only difference is that my idols are not made of wood or stone. But they are idols just the same because they cause my focus to be taken off my God. I worship my desires more than my God.

For example, it may be a temptation to spend God's tithe on a piece of jewelry for myself. It may be the temptation to ignore a person's cry for help when I'm tired, or to fail to uplift someone else who needs encouragement for their rebellious teenager or troubled marriage. It may be a temptation to exaggerate my story to make myself look superior in someone else's estimation. Or it may be a sinful fantasy that, I must honestly admit, I'd enjoy experiencing in reality. Whatever it might be, it's an idol, and it must be torn down.

Do you remember the account of God asking Abraham to sacrifice Isaac? The report is found in Genesis 22. God promised Abraham that his seed would be as great in number as the sand of the sea. Abraham waited for many years and decided to take the matter into his own hands. Ishmael, Abraham's son, was born to his maidservant Hagar. But God intended for Sarah, Abraham's wife, to bear a son. When Isaac was born, Abraham was one hundred years old. God knew that Abraham's love was greater for Isaac than for Himself, so He put Abraham to the test.

When God told Abraham to climb Mount Moriah and sacrifice Isaac, Abraham obeyed God and put Isaac on the altar. When he drew his knife to slay Isaac, an angel appeared. "Abraham! Abraham! Do not lay a hand on the boy. Do not do anything to him. Now I know that you fear God, because you have not withheld from me your son, your only son."

Often I have to climb Mount Moriah, and like Abraham I must make a sacrifice. But when I draw my knife to kill my idol, no angel comes to stop me as he did Abraham with Isaac. Every idol that comes between my God and me *must* be slaughtered.

Then I shift to the New Testament and find

out what Jesus' character looks like. The more
time I spend with Him, looking at His profile, the
more I will become like Him. God created me to
be a reflection of His Son Jesus Christ. My heart is
focused with the clear goal of becoming more like
Jesus.

LISTENING TO GOD

The fourth step in focusing my heart is listening
to God through the Scriptures. What does He
have to say to me, personally, today?

The most meaningful method of listening to
God that I have encountered is meditating in the
Scriptures. This means taking a bit of Scripture
and pondering it, praying over it, thinking about
it, perhaps writing about it — and then applying
it to my life TODAY.

Briefly, the method I have used for over twelve
years is as follows. First I pray and ask God to
direct my thinking. I ask Him to show me what
He has for me today in this particular passage of
Scripture. I open the Scriptures (I begin at the
beginning of a book of the Bible and work
through it systematically), I write down a portion
of it, and then I write the thoughts that come to
my mind relating to that Scripture.

I want to make something very clear at this point: These are thoughts from my *mind* that God has illumined. My writing is not anything occultish like automatic writing, nor is it an aimless movement of my hand as with some "game" boards. Neither is my writing a method of the "New Age" movement. I simply have asked my heavenly Father to fill my mind with His thoughts. If I ask my father for a fish, will He give me a stone? Certainly not our Heavenly Father.

I could tell you of countless times when God directed me through His Word to some area in my life that needed to be changed, or about other times when He encouraged me in some discouraging period in my life, or mornings when He changed the direction in which I was headed. These experiences came as a direct result of being open to listening to what God had to say to me through the Scriptures that day.

I have been meditating in the Scriptures in this manner for sixteen years, and I can tell you from experience, *it works.*

The first time I meditated in this way I didn't know the value of writing out my thoughts, so I cannot quote them exactly. But I will give you the essence, for I remember it well. I prayed and asked God to show me in what book I should begin. The first epistle of Peter came to mind, and so I began there:

> Peter, an apostle of Jesus Christ, to God's elect, strangers in the world, scattered throughout Pontus, Galatia, Cappadocia, Asia and Bithynia, who have been chosen according to the foreknowledge of God the Father...

First of all I remembered Peter. He was impetuous and usually spoke before he thought, so he often had his "foot in his mouth." And Peter was highly opinionated. I identified with each of those traits.

But of all the disciples, he most adamantly pledged loyalty and love to Jesus. Similarly, I declared my discipleship to Jesus.

Then I imagined my Lord asking me a question, even as He had Peter: "Do you love Me?" I answered, "Yes, Lord, You know that I love You." His reply seemed to be, "Then feed My lambs." Again, in my mind, He asked me if I truly loved Him. Like Peter, I replied, "Yes, Lord, You know that I love You." And again the response, "Take care of My sheep." Yet a third time He asked me, "Cheryl Biehl, do you love

Me?" And like Peter I became defensive: "Lord, You know all things; You know that I love You." And He replied, "Feed My sheep."

At that moment I realized what God wanted me to do in this life: I was to teach and feed His children — to disciple women in the things of the Lord. To this day I never, never tire of that. This book is an example of that teaching. I pray it will encourage you to focus on Jesus and to accomplish what would bring you closer to the goal of being "conformed to the likeness of his Son" (Romans 8:29).

Just last week I was leading a small discussion group of women at our church. It was my privilege to sit on the floor in the circle with the "lambs" (the newer Christians). I was explaining the fall of Adam and how that, because of his fall, we are born into that same fallen state. But Jesus became the *new* Adam. As we are "born again" not only are our sins forgiven, but His righteousness is credited to our account.

After this explanation, Nancy looked at me thoughtfully and said, "The lights just came on. I have never understood that before. For the first time it makes sense to me."

One of the greatest thrills of my life is to feed

the lambs and see them digest the food. It truly was an evidence of God's grace that He allowed me to be a part of that process in that beautiful lady's life.

Peter was writing to people in a wide variety of places. I couldn't even pronounce the names of those cities, but God showed me that my ministry would go beyond my local church to other cities and countries. That has proven to be the case, both with my speaking and writing.

Another example I will share with you comes from meditating in the book of Nehemiah. Oh, how I learned to love that book! I'll give you a brief background: Nehemiah was the cupbearer to the king. This meant he tasted the wine before the king did so that if it were poisonous, he would die and not the king! How would you like that job? (But his fringe benefits were substantial; read the book to see how well the king treated him.)

It was a capital offense to come before the king with a sad face, but Nehemiah had just heard of Jerusalem's wall being in a state of great disrepair and he couldn't fake a smile to save himself. Let's pick up on the conversation between Nehemiah and the king. The king begins:

"Why does your face look so sad when you are not ill? This can be nothing but sadness of heart."

I was very much afraid, but said to the king, "May the king live forever! Why should my face not look sad when the city where my fathers are buried lies in ruins, and its gates have been destroyed by fire?"

The king said to me, "What is it you want?" (Nehemiah 2:2-4)

The portion of Scripture I was to meditate on that day was this last sentence: "The king said to me, 'What is it you want?'"

It was as if my King, my Heavenly Father, asked me, "Cheryl, what do you want from Me?" I thought and wrote for perhaps an hour. I recalled how Hannah wanted a baby boy; Solomon asked for wisdom; Esther asked for favor from her husband, the king; and David asked that one of his descendants would sit on the throne forever.

But what did *I* want? What was the most important thing I could ask for from my God in this life? After much thought and, I believe, after

God put the desire within my heart, I concluded that what I wanted most from God was to know Him. Then and there it was clear to me what my purpose was in life: to know God. There could be no other answer for me.

Today I study the Scriptures to know Him. I read to find out what insights others have gained in their pursuit of knowing Him. I love to be in the presence of people who teach me more about Him. I long for the day when I will know Him perfectly, even as I am known... when I will see Him face to face.

Please understand that I am not suggesting that every person needs to spend the same amount of time I do going before God; nor am I suggesting that everyone should seek His guidance in the same way I do. If you are a mother of four preschoolers, perhaps the time of fewest distractions for you — the time when you can most easily focus on God — is in the shower. The amount of time, the hour of the day, and the methods you use may vary throughout your lifetime. Find the best time, place, and methods for you.*

* You may study further about meditating on the Bible in my book *Scriptural Meditation* (revised edition ©1989), published by Questar Publishers, Inc.

Before going on, I suggest that you write out here what YOU would ask from God.

_____

_____

_____

_____

USING A PRAYER NOTEBOOK

After I've focused my heart on God and read and meditated in His Word, I open my prayer notebook.

Perhaps, like me, you can recall talking with a friend who shared a request that you promised to bring before the Father in prayer — but for which, in your busy schedule, you forgot to pray. And then, some time later that friend thanked you for praying, because God had answered her in an unusual way. If so, you felt embarrassed and ashamed as I did, because you hadn't remembered to pray at all. Creating and *using* a system of writing down prayer requests in a notebook lessens the likelihood of that happening.

This tool should never be considered a "gimme" list. Some argue that a prayer notebook is a little like handing God a grocery list. I agree that it easily can be that meaningless. And I do use a prayer notebook for the same reason I have a grocery list: I simply can't remember everything without one. But I don't go to the grocery store, hand the manager my list, then return to my car to read a book while he collects the items on my list and puts them in my trunk. NO! I hold the list in my hand, walk through the aisles, and pull the items off the shelves myself.

The same is true with my prayer list. I don't just hand my list to God; I pray through it, asking God to make each person whom I present to Him in prayer to become more like Jesus in and through his or her present circumstances. I ask Him to change some of the difficult situations these people face, if such a change would be His perfect will.

Don't ever believe that just writing down a request means you have prayed for it. Some people think that God looks at their notebook daily, and that therefore the time it takes to write down a request is all the time they need to spend on it; their obligation is complete. No! You write it down to *remind you to pray* for it.

There are many ways to organize a prayer notebook. Some people use a clean page for each day's requests. Others have separate pages for praise, confession, intercession (praying for the needs of others) and petition (praying for your own needs).

The method that has been most helpful to me is a yearly notebook that designates a separate page for each person for whom I pray. I put his or her name at the top of the page, then list general requests I have for him or her, requests that will continue to be answered throughout life.

For instance, I pray that my husband would have God's wisdom in his life. Even though I see consistent evidences of that wisdom, there will never be a day when I can say, "It is settled forever; my husband has perfect and complete godly wisdom."

I pray for myself to be a godly woman. And I pray to know God. But those prayers will never be *completely* answered until I stand before Jesus face to face.

These are general requests. I have perhaps four or five of them for each person.

Then I begin listing specific requests, the answers to which can be measured and dated. Requests for health, for successful appointments, houses to sell, safe trips, and so on, can all be answered yes or no.

I divide the page in half vertically with an imaginary line. On the left side I put the date and the specific request. When the request is answered, I record the date and the specific answer on the same line as the request, but on the right half of the page.

I also have preferential ordering of names in my notebook. As much as I'd like to, I don't pray *all* the way through my notebook *every* day. There are certain people for whom I believe I have a greater responsibility to pray than others. My family is first, so I pray for them first.

People with a large number of others for whom to pray, or whose time is especially limited, often find it helpful to divide their prayer notebook into sections by days. Besides a daily prayer list (which would include their family and others who are particularly close), they have a list marked "Monday" which might include our country's political leaders. On Tuesday they might concentrate their prayer on leaders and teachers in the church. Wednesday's list would focus on missionaries, and so on.

There are some days when I am able to spend an hour or more praying; other days I can pray only a few minutes. On some days I spend more time meditating in the Scriptures, and on other days more time is spent petitioning for the needs of those for whom I believe God would have me pray. There's no set time formula for me.

You may ask, "How do you decide whose names go into your prayer notebook?" I've already mentioned that my family is included. Also listed are:

- my pastor and his family
- other church staff and their families
- current requests I know of within the church
- close friends and acquaintances, and their families
- friends of my children
- our country and her leaders — the president, and members of Congress
- whomever God puts on my heart.

As I pray through my notebook, seeing answers to prayer gives me great cause to be thankful. Satan, the enemy of my soul, used to raise questions in my mind as to the validity of my prayers, and caused me to question if God in fact really answered them. This doesn't happen anymore because I have pages from years past as well as the current year with the right half completed — concrete proof of answers to prayer.

In early January I start a new notebook with fresh pages, simply transferring unanswered requests to the next year. I have saved over fifteen years' worth of prayer notebooks. What a reminder of the faithfulness of our God!

My family knows that upon my death, they are to sort the pages by person and give them to the people for whom I have prayed. I hope it will be an encouragement to all of them to know how God's hand was upon them in answering prayer on their behalf.

A prayer notebook is only one of many tools which may help you to remember to bring a request before God. If your life is filled with caring for small children, a more effective reminder may be to place notes — saying, "Pray for Robin," for example — on the mirror in the bathroom or on the wall above the changing table. Be creative in finding methods which best suit your situation.

Perhaps you don't need a reminder. God blessed Shari with such an incredible memory that she doesn't even need a grocery list. If that is the case, you may not need a prayer notebook to remind you of specific requests. But the encouragement of logging answers may be the benefit you need to justify the time it takes to record those specific requests and answers.

When selecting a notebook, you may find a looseleaf better than a spiral because it's easier to insert added pages as prayer requests grow and answers are given.

READING FROM A DAILY STUDY

I also like to read from a daily study each morning. I suggest you choose one which will challenge your thinking, such as Ligonier Valley Study Center's *Tabletalk*(a free copy is available from Tabletalk, P.O. Box 547500, Orlando, FL 32854-9989, telephone 1-800-435-4343). Another is *Daily Secrets of Christian Living* by George Mueller (and compiled by Al Bryant), or Oswald Chamber's classic daily study, *My Utmost for His Highest*. Many others also are available. It's good discipline for you to exercise our "gray matter" and do some theological thinking. As you read these studies, however, don't just blindly accept what others teach. Search the Scriptures yourself to find answers.

Depending on your particular season and circumstances of life, consider the study possibilities before you. You may want to work through a tape series or some challenging book. At a time in my life when I had considerable uncommitted time to devote to such pursuits, I completed a long and extensive tape series on systematic theology taught by Dr. R.C. Sproul. This series stands out as a diamond in the broach containing the gems I've collected in my lifetime. I'm so grateful God gave me the time to complete that outstanding series.

RESTING IN GOD'S SOVEREIGNTY

The final part of focusing your heart and mind is to rest in God's sovereignty, and be at peace within it. Remember that He is in absolute control and will work out *everything* in your life for His ultimate purpose — which is to conform you to His image (Romans 8:28-29). Focus on Him, pray for direction, and rest in Him, knowing that He will direct you according to His perfect will.

In times of greatest personal stress and anxiety, I fall back on words which have been of great personal help to me, words written by Helmut Thielicke in *Life Can Begin Again*. (I encourage you to purchase and read this classic book based on the Sermon on the Mount.) In a chapter titled "Overcoming Anxiety," his perspective is insightful and persuasive in helping me release anxiety to God. If space permitted I would quote the chapter in its entirety, but will settle for one paragraph:

We are not carefree when the sea is calm and the ship of our life glides pleasantly along. But we can be carefree even if the waves rise high, when the Lord sleeps in our ship and we know that it cannot go down, that winds and weather cannot hurt us, because he who can command them in a moment is with us. The one care that should concern us is that we do not throw away our trust in the Lord, who would sleep in our ship and is able to walk upon the waves. As soon as we direct our cares to the wrong address, namely, the waves, we are caught in the grip of mortal terror and we sink just as Peter did. False care is not to be combatted with an artificial and forced carefreeness — this would be sterile make-believe and would lead to nothing but an ostrich policy. Care can only be cured by care. Care about many things can be cured only by care about "the one thing needful." This is the homeopathy of divine healing.

Several years ago Bobb and I were privileged to listen to Dr. R.C. Sproul give a message at the Crystal Cathedral in Anaheim, California. He declared, "There is not one single, solitary, maverick molecule outside of God's sovereign control." That evening Bobb and I reflected on this awesome truth.

Months later, we were in deep emotional pain, feeling from a human level that situations in which we were intimately involved were utterly out of control. As we lay in bed one night, Bobb took my hand and said to me, "Cheryl, remember that there is not one maverick molecule outside of God's sovereign control." Tears of relief flooded my pillow as my focus shifted from how great the problem was to how much greater my God is.

Are you facing a dilemma even now that seems unsolvable? An obstacle that seems insurmountable? A pit out of which you cannot seem to climb? Focus your eyes on how big God is rather than how big the difficulty appears. He is unequivocally sovereign, and the absolute truth is that there are no maverick molecules outside of His control. Put your trust in Him. If you are His child, He will work within the situation for your ultimate good.

How do you balance your heart and mind? Focus on Jesus. Allow HIM to establish for you a perspective of who God is, who you are, and where you fit in the broad scope of eternity.

DISCUSSION QUESTIONS

1. How do you picture God as you imagine approaching His throne?

2. What "tools" do you use to remember prayer requests?

3. If God asked you what you most wanted from Him, how would you answer?

4. Take a few minutes to meditate on Deuteronomy 31:8: "The Lord himself goes before you and will be with you; he will never leave you nor forsake you. Do not be afraid; do not be discouraged." Share your thoughts with others.

2

Establishing Your Priorities

ON THE WALLS of our guest powder room hang lovingly restored pictures of my maternal ancestors. If you visited my home I would tell you stories from all their histories, as well as precisely where each one fits in the roots of my lineage. Grandma Frances Shupe was the only one I knew personally, but I am confident that if I had known each of them, she still would have been my favorite. The impact she had on my life is immeasurable because I spent countless hours with her in priceless companionship.

Today I cherish the mantle clock she gave me. It had been a wedding gift to her from her husband's parents. I also have her quilt, which hangs on the wall above our bed, a hand-cut cobalt crystal candy dish I meticulously chose and purchased in Germany with the inheritance she left me, a *Memories* album which she completed with the help of my patient father, and many other invaluable heirlooms.

Grandma Shupe was ninety-six years old when the angels came to carry her to her heavenly mansion. On earth she left behind her an extraordinary spiritual heritage and the legacy of a model life to emulate.

I remember Thanksgiving dinners at her home in Bad Axe, Michigan. The extended family gathered annually for true thanksgiving to God for a year of prosperity. The twenty-foot-long table was filled to capacity, with turkey, chicken, pumpkin pie, mincemeat pie, carrot pudding, five vegetables, two kinds of potatoes, cranberry salad, four kinds of pickles, pickled beets, and all the traditional trimmings. The smells from her kitchen still linger in my memory. Oh yes, I must mention that her candy dish was always filled and refilled with chocolate-covered peanuts.

I could never hope to fill her saintly shoes, but the challenge now is mine on Thanksgiving Day to attempt to duplicate her feast. I feel especially close to her in the days preceding the celebration dinner. My kitchen bustles with the preparation just as hers once did. Magically, at 2:30 P.M. that day, everything is cooked to perfection, carved, and ready to serve at the ideal temperature.

Several years ago when I reached to seize the proverbial baton of this Thanksgiving tradition as it left Grandma's hand, I sat down and did some serious planning. First I recalled and recorded the menu. Second I composed the grocery list, then the activity list, and finally a time-line for completing each particular action.

My planning began at the *end*. By 2:30 on Thanksgiving Day I wanted to have the entire meal on the table. To do that I obviously needed to accomplish all food preparation before that time. The family was invited to help as they wish, but everything had to be prepared in my kitchen (admittedly selfish, I won't share those smells with anyone else's kitchen). According to the schedule, at 2:20 the glasses are filled with water, and the parade of food to the table begins. Prior to that, at 2:15, the food is put into serving dishes. At 2:10 the turkey is carved, and so on.

If I waited until noon on Thursday to begin the dinner, it wouldn't be served by 2:30. If I didn't have a detailed plan of action, the green beans and the rice pudding wouldn't be ready to come off the stove and out of the oven simultaneously.

Just as such a dinner must be planned in advance with precision and painstaking strategy, so it is with the rest of life. If you wait until you're seventy-five to decide what you want to accomplish in your lifetime, you'll come up short in the time required to turn your dreams into reality.

The first thing I suggest you do is thoughtfully decide (1) what or who you want to *be*, (2) who or what you want to *help* (3) what you want to *do*, and (4) what you want to *have* before you die. Then I'll show you how to work backward to plan your life so you can actually realize those intentions.

BEFORE YOU DIE...

Later in this chapter you will find a "LIFE FOCUS" chart. I urge you to take the time necessary to complete it as accurately and thoroughly as you possibly can. I suggest you use pencil to make changes easier and to give you freedom to write down ideas that you don't set as goals now but which may blossom into genuine desires and plans later.

I have completed a sample chart for you to study first. The sample chart is followed by a blank chart for you to complete.

As you fill in the boxes, keep in mind these seven areas of life:
- Spiritual
- Family/Marriage
- Professional/Mental
- Physical
- Financial
- Personal Development
- Social/Friends.

As a Christian, the Spiritual area infiltrates every part of your life. For instance, because you are a Christian, you must maintain honest relationships in the Professional area. You can never embrace a "dog-eat-dog" mentality to climb the corporate ladder. There is nothing intrinsically wrong with reaching the top rung of that ladder, but to push someone else down to accomplish it is not obeying the biblical mandate to love your neighbor as yourself.

Even though the Spiritual category pervades all the others, it also deserves to be considered separately. One priority you may wish to include in the "DO" column in the Spiritual area may be your desire to read the Bible through systematically from front to back cover. Another priority may be to make a study of what the Bible teaches about grace or fear.

In the Social/Friends category, your list in the

"Do" column might include having an annual Christmas party, or traveling to Europe with a favorite couple. In the "Have" column, you may list several people with whom you would like to become friends. "Help" may include supporting a friend's missionary trip. And "Be" may list a commitment to having a genuine, "fully present" listening ear ready for friends who may be struggling with their children or marriage.

If you're having difficulty coming up with anything to put in the boxes, brainstorm by removing restrictive limits. God doesn't limit our creativity. His purpose for us is to be conformed to His image. Consider His creation and you will conclude that He doesn't desire to restrain or limit our creative abilities. He will stimulate our minds to greater levels than we could ever imagine. You will actually be more fulfilled if you relinquish your desires to His control.

Try to uncover authentic desires within yourself by removing limitations. What would you like to be, do, have, or help with if you had absolutely unlimited funds available, you knew you couldn't fail at whatever you chose to do, and you were responsible to God alone? Removing limitations may stimulate ideas that might otherwise be screened out before entering your conscious mind. Use your mental capacities to formulate a creative plan allowing you to realize the dreams that are most important to you as you seek God's perspective.

You may discover you have a long list in the "Help" column but very little in the "Be" column in the social category, while in the Mental/Professional category the longest list is in the "Do" column. There are no right or wrong answers or correct lengths for these lists. Put down what is important for you. Pray and ask God to show you what would please Him.

Not all the boxes need to be filled out completely. It's perfectly acceptable to leave several blocks blank. Write down your goals in whatever areas are important to you. This chart is simply a vehicle to help you look beyond present circumstances and see a long-term picture of what you'd like to accomplish in your life.

Spend time working and reworking the chart; weigh carefully each item listed. Ask yourself how important this actually is to you. Remember, however, that it's written in pencil; a year, month, or week from now you have the freedom to change it completely if you are exposed to some new and challenging idea, or if the priority you chose has lost its appeal.

LIFE FOCUS

Before I die, I want to...

	BE:	DO:
SPIRITUAL	Focused on God	Summer missionary project Bible study at work
FAMILY/ MARRIAGE	Wife — happily married, Mother of 3 children	Raise the family Support children thru college Family vacations Trip with my parents
PROFESSIONAL/ MENTAL	A nurse	Floor nurse in hospital
PHYSICAL	120 pounds	Aerobics 5 days/week Bicycle trip to San Diego
FINANCIAL	Comfortable Responsible to pay bills Generous	Set up budget & live by it
PERSONAL DEVELOPMENT	An encourager	Learn to ride a horse Learn to speak Spanish Take piano lessons
SOCIAL/ FRIENDS	A good listener to my friends	Lunch 1/wk with a friend Have a Christmas party

LIFE FOCUS

Before I die, I want to…

HAVE:	HELP:	
Daily time of worship & prayer	Pray with hurting patients House unwed girls in crisis pregnancies	SPIRITUAL
"Happy" husband & 3 children	Emotional & physical support for family	FAMILY/ MARRIAGE
Nursing degree	People who are physically hurting	PROFESSIONAL/ MENTAL
Cholesterol level under 200	My family by serving nutritional meals	PHYSICAL
Home paid for	Homeless people Church giving Trust for each grandchild	FINANCIAL
		PERSONAL DEVELOPMENT
	A friend's child on a summer missionary trip	SOCIAL/ FRIENDS

LIFE FOCUS

Before I die, I want to…

	BE:	DO:
SPIRITUAL		
FAMILY/ MARRIAGE		
PROFESSIONAL/ MENTAL		
PHYSICAL		
FINANCIAL		
PERSONAL DEVELOPMENT		
SOCIAL/ FRIENDS		

LIFE FOCUS

Before I die, I want to…

HAVE:	HELP:	
		SPIRITUAL
		FAMILY/ MARRIAGE
		PROFESSIONAL/ MENTAL
		PHYSICAL
		FINANCIAL
		PERSONAL DEVELOPMENT
		SOCIAL/ FRIENDS

CHOOSING LADDERS

As I mentioned in the introduction, this book is a manual to help you sort out what is important to you and then to help you produce a plan to make those things become reality.

Completing the "Life Focus" chart is like looking at different "ladders" to decide which ones you will choose to climb, and which "walls" you'll choose to lean those ladders against. If you don't make those choices, you're likely to find yourself climbing the first ladder you see, and not liking where it took you when you reach the top. You'll regret the effort you spent climbing it.

I suggest you follow Habakkuk's example. Habakkuk was upset because God wasn't answering him in the way or with the timing that Habakkuk thought was best. But Habakkuk knew that if he had a difference with the Almighty, it was a problem with *his* thinking, not God's. So he did a very wise thing: Habakkuk climbed his tower and waited to get God's perspective. Take the time to stop and pray for God to give you His perspective on your life.

It would be so simple if we had the option of calling God up on the phone and asking Him to give us a direct answer about what He would have us do in life. Unfortunately we don't have that option. The truth is, God isn't going to write out your goals for you on tablets of stone, as He wrote His holy laws for Moses.

But He has given us prayer as a means of communication with Him. He has given us Scripture to follow as His written guide. He has given His Holy Spirit to teach us, to remind us of His truths, and to comfort us. And He has given us a brain which He expects us to use.

God has promised that if we go before Him and sincerely ask for His wisdom, He will give it to us. James 1:5 gives us direction with a promise: "If any of you lacks wisdom, he should ask God, who gives generously to all without finding fault, and it will be given to him." Proverbs encourages us to make plans, counting on God to direct us.

Search the Scriptures to determine if they speak directly to a particular issue in question. You also may seek the counsel of Christians who are more mature in their faith than you are.

If God is sovereign, He can certainly redirect us if He has something for us to do other than what we are planning. For instance, the apostle Paul planned several times to go to Rome and each time was prevented from doing so. When he finally arrived, he was a prisoner in chains. Paul was listening to God, and so must you.

Pray sincerely, seeking God's will — then proceed, always open and willing to be flexible and pliable in the hand of God.

Working through the "Life Focus" chart will help you achieve maximum benefit from this book. Complete the chart before proceeding further in the book. If you read ahead without actually participating in the assignments, it may be confusing or overwhelming to you. The temptation will be to put the book down and give up. Fill out the chart one step at a time as you choose which ladders you will climb.

WHOSE FOCUS?

An interesting cultural transition has occurred in the last thirty to forty years. Some of you who are reading this book were taught by your parents and culture that the man of the home was to "bring home the bacon" while the wife stayed home, raised babies, cooked the family meals, and sewed the clothing, never leaving the house except to grocery shop, never voicing an opinion, and certainly never making an independent decision.

Today our culture suggests that two self-reliant people can live under the same roof, financially independent of each other. While they may be raising children, marriage is an option to be discussed and decided upon. If they are married, they are in reality married singles.

These scenarios are the extremes. But within those frameworks lie countless balances that must be determined by each couple. Questions soon arise: Who should determine your life's focus, and how independently should you establish them? For some of you who are married it would be unthinkable to complete the chart alone; you would feel comfortable only if your husband did it for you. Others of you (both single and married) will determine all of it independently, while most of you will utilize a blending of ideas: Some personal goals you'll set on your own, while setting family goals together with your husband. Only you can sort out those issues. The Bible teaches that "the two shall be one," and as Christian women we must follow that biblical mandate. Go before God and ask Him to give you direction.

If you are married, you are a part of a family unit which works together. It is not wrong to experience independent areas of fulfillment, but you are responsible before God to complete the obligations of your role within the family. You are to contribute to unity rather than divisiveness or autonomy within the family unit. If you find that your goals are undermining the well-being of the family, you must be willing to alter or postpone your goals for the good of the whole family.

Again, go before God and sincerely seek His will for your life. Gain His perspective!

SEASONS OF LIFE

Below I have listed eleven possible seasons through which you may pass in your lifetime. I do not claim this to be an exhaustive list. You may find yourself in more than one season at the same time, or you may skip a season altogether and move into the next one. (On this list, ~~cross out~~ the seasons through which you have already passed, and place a check mark (✓) beside the season(s) in which you now find yourself:)

__ 1. Childhood

__ 2. Adolescence

__ 3. Single Adulthood

__ 4. Married without Children

__ 5. Family with Preschool Children

__ 6. Family with School-age Children

___ 7. Family with Teenage Children

___ 8. Empty Nester

___ 9. Grandparent

___ 10. Caring for Elderly Parent(s)

___ 11. Widowhood

Two other "seasons" must also be included in this list. These may intrude into several of the seasons listed above, so I will not list them in any sequential order:

___ • Single Parenthood

___ • Blended Family

Not everyone passes through each season of life. You may, for instance, remain single throughout your adult lifetime. This affords options to you that married people don't have, because you have different responsibilities.

The apostle Paul said singleness was a better way to live because the single person seeks to please God alone, rather than her family. As a single you can define what you would like to do without regarding the needs of others for whom you are responsible or to whom you are accountable.

If you have children, they will require different kinds and amounts of dedicated time from you, their mother, according to their ages. In the early school years you may be a room mother, which requires a commitment of perhaps one day a month for chaperoning a field trip or class party. When your children are in their later elementary and junior high grades, you may become their "cheerleader" at various sporting events, requiring your attendance at practices or games several days each week.

When your children move into adolescence, you expend much emotional and physical energy as you seek to help them bridge the gap between childhood and adulthood. Confusion is normal as they cut the "apron strings" and gain independence, while at the same time trying to understand who this person is who is living inside their rapidly changing body. You need to commit time to your children in this season in an effort to help them through this difficult and often frustrating process.

You may find that the "empty-nester" season has a "revolving door." Perhaps your children will return temporarily, or maybe your parents will move into your home in their final years. Grandchildren may cause laughter to bounce off the walls of your home.

Even though widowhood is not an eagerly

anticipated season, statistics from the U.S. Department of Health reveal that, on the average, women outlive their husbands by seven years. Listing options which would interest you, should you ever find yourself in that station, may help your adjustment.

I am not suggesting that carrying out these options would eliminate your grief. You should never repress or deny such feelings. Jesus Himself wept when Lazarus died. If your deceased husband was a believer in Jesus, he is far better off than any situation this world could offer, but you will miss him, and experiencing genuine grief at your loss is healthy. Being able, however, to look at future options during this very difficult time may help you focus your energies beyond the immediate situation and actually aid in the healing process.

In our society today, husbands often put pressure on us to work outside the home. Let's examine several reasons why this coercion often occurs. If you find yourself in this situation, consider that perhaps your husband is attempting to be sensitive to you, believing you would enjoy the stimulation that working outside the home may afford you. He may see career women at his office who seem fulfilled and happy, and he may be thinking, "I know my wife could do that too. I'll bet she'd like the challenge and social interaction that come with a career outside the home."

On the other hand, he actually may think you are being lethargic, and fears you may not be living up to your full potential.

Whatever his reason, if your desire at this point is not to work, show him your seasonal goals. Point out what you believe is critical to the best interest of the family at this time, and show him that you have a plan for when the present situation changes. This may diminish his apprehensions.

On the following pages you will find "SEASONS OF LIFE" charts. First there is a sample for you to review in helping you complete your own chart, which follows. Remember to use pencil so you can exercise the freedom to change your mind as new information occurs in your life.

At the heading of the first column in the blank chart, just to the right of the words "Season of Life," write in the season of life in which you currently find yourself. At the top of the other columns, write in the future seasons in which you eventually expect to be.

Beneath each heading, you will write in goals from your "Life Focus" chart which you completed earlier. (Study the sample "Season in Life" chart for ideas and clarification.) Notice how the "Life Focus" sample goals are woven into the seasonal chart.)

Look back at your completed "Life Focus" chart. Which aspirations listed there are feasible for you to accomplish in the season of life in which you currently find yourself? Choose the ambitions which are most meaningful to you now, and place them in the first blank chart. Select other goals which would be best to accomplish later, and list them under the season of life which best fits each goal. Repeat the process until all of the priorities listed in your "Life Focus" chart have found a box in your "Seasons of Life" chart, in whichever season they best fit. (Again, use the sample chart to find examples of how this process works.)

This process can easily be compared to a college student deciding her major, visiting her counselor to obtain a list of the necessary classes she must take to secure her degree, and then deciding in which semester she will take each of those classes. Of course, she will shuffle that plan many times to accommodate things which are

unforeseen when her original blueprint was
drawn. But she has a plan, and she knows that if
she takes certain courses in specified semesters,
she is on her way to satisfying the requirements
for her diploma.

As you work on these charts, seek God's
direction. Ask Him to show you what is best for
you and what you can do to become more like
Him. He tells us that as we are open to His
leading, He will give us the desires of our heart.
He puts desires within us and then gives us the
joy of seeing them realized. You will probably
discover that a few of those things you listed will
eventually lose their importance. Others will gain
value.

Perhaps frustrations will be relieved and
contentment increased as you come to notice that
you are not giving up things which are
meaningful to you, but only postponing them for
a later season of your life. For instance, when I
had preschool children, I knew that someday I
would like to write and speak, but this was not
best at that time; those ambitions had to wait
until the "empty-nester" season of my life. I
didn't feel cheated that I couldn't realize those
goals during that season because I strongly
believed the most important role I could play in

my life at that time was to be a loving and caring mother to my children.

I didn't resent playing with Bozo, Barbie dolls, or tractors because they weren't robbing me of anything else I wanted to do right then. I genuinely wanted to be playing with our children, teaching them about Jesus and about how to live in this world. At the time I knew my books and speaking could wait until our children were older, when it would actually be physically more comfortable to sit at a computer and write than to crawl on the floor pushing a fire engine.

Don't eliminate your aspirations simply because you aren't able to accomplish them right now. Carefully choose the season of life in which they most logically fit, and find satisfaction in achieving the goals you choose for today.

SEASONS OF LIFE

SEASON> OF LIFE	FAMILY WITH PRESCHOOL CHILDREN	FAMILY WITH TEENAGE CHILDREN
SPIRITUAL	Focused on God Attend morning Bible study 1/wk 30 min. personal time with God each day	Focused on God 45 minutes personal time with God each day
FAMILY/ MARRIAGE	Family vacations	Family vacations
PROFESSIONAL/ MENTAL	Take 2 classes per term toward RN degree	Take 2 classes per term toward RN degree
PHYSICAL	Aerobics 3 days per week	Aerobics 5 days per week Bicycle trip to San Diego
FINANCIAL	Give tithe to church Savings for children's college	Give tithe to church Savings for children's college
PERSONAL DEVELOPMENT	Learn to ride a horse Take piano lessons with children	Learn to speak Spanish with children Take piano lessons with children
SOCIAL/ FRIENDS	Dinner & evening with friends 1/month	

SEASONS OF LIFE

EMPTY NESTER	GRANDCHILDREN	<SEASON OF LIFE
Focused on God Summer missionary project House unwed mothers 1 hr. daily personal time w/God	Focused on God Pray with hurting patients 1 hr. daily personal time w/God	SPIRITUAL

Support children through
    college
Trip with my parents
	Trip with children & grand-
	    children
		FAMILY/
		MARRIAGE

Finish RN degree Work in hospital	Become floor nurse	PROFESSIONAL/ MENTAL
Aerobics 5 days per week	Walk 3 miles per day	PHYSICAL

Finish paying for home before
    retirement
Give tithe, plus extra projects
	Finish paying for home before
	    retirement
	Give tithe, plus extra projects
	Buy bonds for each grandchild
		FINANCIAL

		PERSONAL DEVELOPMENT
Lunch once a week with a friend Have a Christmas party	Lunch once a week with a friend Support a friend's child in a missionary project	SOCIAL/ FRIENDS

SEASONS OF LIFE

SEASON> OF LIFE		
SPIRITUAL		
FAMILY/ MARRIAGE		
PROFESSIONAL/ MENTAL		
PHYSICAL		
FINANCIAL		
PERSONAL DEVELOPMENT		
SOCIAL/ FRIENDS		

SEASONS OF LIFE

		<SEASON OF LIFE
		SPIRITUAL
		FAMILY/ MARRIAGE
		PROFESSIONAL/ MENTAL
		PHYSICAL
		FINANCIAL
		PERSONAL DEVELOPMENT
		SOCIAL/ FRIENDS

GOOD VS. BEST

If you feel overwhelmed by the number of interests you have and are experiencing the "I can't do everything" syndrome, take time to sort out the difference between the good and the best.

We will look more carefully at this distinction as we move into the next chapters. For now, let me say that you *can't* do everything, but you *can* do what is best and most important for you. Few of us are tempted to allow bad things to keep us from achieving the best, but good things certainly can and do often consume our time, robbing us of what we want to do most. Weigh each item you listed on the "Life Focus" chart. Is it a "good" or a "best" for you?

In Philippians 1:9-11, Paul tells the saints in Philippi of his prayer for them:

> And this is my prayer: that your love may abound more and more in knowledge and depth of insight, so that you may be able to discern what is best and may be pure and blameless until the day of Christ, filled with the fruit of righteousness that comes through Jesus Christ—to the glory and praise of God.

Paul's prayer for them is that they would be able to discern what is "best" for them. How were they to determine that? By letting their love abound more and more in knowledge and depth of insight. In other words, by seeking God's face they would gain insight and know what was the best for them. How would that benefit them? It would cause them to be pure and blameless until the day of Christ, filled with the fruit of right-eousness. If we always choose what is best, we will be pure and blameless.

Again, let me emphasize that this is a personal value judgment and can only be deter-mined *for* you *by* you. An ambition which is a "best" for you may be a "good" for someone else, and vice versa. Something which is only a "good" for you in one season of your life may be a "best" for you in another.

In the future, when experiences of life may seem unfulfilling, remember this exercise. Recall that there was a day when you looked down the continuum of seasons in your future and carefully chose the "bests" for yourself as a Christian woman. You will be doing things because they are what you determined then were actually what you most wanted to do.

Other seasons in your future will afford you

opportunities to achieve goals that you are currently postponing but not eliminating. It may seem now that those future seasons, when you look forward to having more time and more options, will never come. But I'll tell you from experience, they seem to happen overnight. Don't rob yourself of the joy of this season by wishing you were in a future or past one. Each season has its unique value; focus on present possibilities, and be content with today. Live each day to its fullest.

DISCUSSION QUESTIONS:

1. Give an example from your life where you can work a time-line backwards in order to accomplish a goal.

2. If you are married, how would you describe the relationship you have with your husband in regard to setting your own goals versus fitting into his?

3. As you completed your "Life Focus" chart, did anything emerge from your subconscious thinking which you had not been aware was even a desire? If so, what?

4. After completing your "Seasons of Life" chart, are you fully satisfied with what you are doing in this particular season of your life, realizing that other seasons will afford you different options and opportunities?

3

Setting Your Goals

THIRTEEN PEOPLE gathered one evening in our living room in response to God's having led Denny Bellesi and his wife Leesa to start a church in the Laguna area, where we live. We discussed whether those present were prepared to pledge ourselves to such a commitment. Several people declined; others joined those of us who answered affirmatively, and today, a few short years later, we are witnessing tremendous evidence of God's blessing. Because Denny remains faithful in preaching God's Word, every week people come to Christ and grow in their faith.

In the church's third year, Denny approached me about becoming director of women's ministries. I explained that my schedule was filled, though I was honored that he would consider me for the position. I knew I would thoroughly enjoy the challenge, and my heart was screaming "yes"; but at that point in my life I had to decline.

Denny prayed for this position to be filled, and God increased my burden to feed those sheep. After he approached me the third time in a two-month period, I went back to the place where you are now — of fitting goals into my life — and I reevaluated the situation.

Being an empty nester, I had no children at home who might be robbed of my attention; also, Bobb traveled a considerable amount, affording me necessary time flexibility. However, I worked in his office almost double full-time hours, and wore the hats of office manager, accountant, travel agent, self-taught in-house computer specialist, and any other hat which showed up on my hall tree needing a head to support it.

I evaluated and reevaluated my priorities and seasonal goals. Would this opportunity be a "good" robbing me of a "best," or was this the "best" for me at this point in life? My heart pulled me toward those women, since I understood a bit of what could be accomplished in our church through the women's ministry. Yet I feared my husband might think me disloyal if I abandoned him in the office. I knew he depended on me, and my love for him would not allow me to make him my second priority. I wrestled with the decision, inwardly torn by what seemed to me to be two mutually exclusive "bests." I cried out to God, *"I can't do everything!"* and prayed for wisdom.

Then an idea came to me: If I effectively delegated responsibilities of both the women's ministries and my work at the office, I could accomplish my goals in each area. I prayed for help, then labored over the church directory to find God's perfect choice to chair each particular division of the women's ministry. Carefully I chose a team of strong, creative, and capable women. (I affectionately call them the "Wonder Women.") They eagerly agreed to help me but had no interest in having the proverbial "buck" stop with them. Now that I hold the title of Director of Women's Ministries, I encourage them to delegate similarly so that none of us experiences the burn-out syndrome.

This leadership team meets monthly to pray together, brainstorm for the future, report progress, discuss policies, and to encourage, support, love, and stimulate one another.

As I write this, we just experienced our annual "Christmas Street" boutique. Please indulge me by letting me tell you how extraordinary it was.

Our purpose was threefold: (1) an outreach to the community; (2) an opportunity for women to earn money as they worked throughout the year to make saleable craft items without needing to take a job outside their home, and (3) a painless way to underwrite funds for special women's events we plan to host in the future.

This project fell under the division of "Outreach," which Bonnie and Marlene co-chair. Since Marlene's efforts were committed to the women's retreat, Bonnie accepted the torch for the boutique. She recruited Lorie, who in turn recruited a fantastic committee.

If anyone came up with a feasible suggestion, our response was, "That's a fabulous idea; will you head a committee and make it happen?" And so it went, many hands making lighter work.

Over five hundred women came through the doors of a beautiful home that a generous family in our church allowed us to use. Many of these ladies had never been to our church, but each of them will receive a note of appreciation for stopping by, along with an invitation to join us for our Christmas Eve services at a local resort hotel. Our prayer is that as many come and hear the Christmas message, they will be drawn to our Savior, whose birth we celebrate. The first goal was met… we certainly had an outreach to our community.

Thirty-seven women brought an amazingly high quality of goods to sell at the boutique. Stories are numerous of women who sold everything they brought, allowing them to pay bills or providing a much more abundant Christmas for their family. Financial needs were met. Goal number two: mission accomplished.

With some of the money we collected for the church, we have provided scholarships for the women's retreat, our next project. Some will go to supplement payments to baby sitters who are provided for mothers who attend weekly Bible studies or support groups. Some of the money raised will underwrite a fall fashion show (another outreach to the community). We're going to the "highways and byways" inviting people to come to Christ in the most creative ways we can. So our third goal — to underwrite other women's ministry projects — was reached and exceeded beyond our dreams.

Back to the boutique: My heart was overwhelmed with joy as I went from room to room, checkbook in hand, buying Christmas presents and watching as relationships deepened between vendors throughout the day. I saw smiles exchanged between strangers, and people affirmed in their creative abilities. My un-churched friend was shopping, feeling very comfortable. I pray she comes to the Christmas Eve service and feels so welcome there that she will eventually come to church.

A most satisfying thought came to me: I hadn't attended a single committee meeting for the boutique, but I knew that because I sought wisdom from God two years ago, made a commitment, and prayed as He put the team together, significant things were happening within the lives of women in our church. I have no doubt that God wants me to serve Him in this place in this season of my life.

Denny came through those doors of the boutique to observe, encourage, and bless the people. I'm sure his thoughts were similar to mine; because he had obeyed God and moved a hundred miles from where he called home, God is blessing and changing lives. God shows us His grace when He allows us to experience the joy of being involved in His work.

If directional goals had not been set, people wouldn't have known where to commit their energies, and the levels of achievement we are experiencing would never have been attained.

FORMING YOUR GOALS

YOU'VE ALREADY ESTABLISHED your personal focus before God and determined general priorities in seasonal categories of your life. The next step is to set some goals.

Goals are **realistic, measurable targets for the future.** Let's study that definition carefully.

DEFINING GOALS

Goals are *realistic.* Perhaps in the past you have failed at achieving a goal; so, just as with New Year's Resolutions, you now avoid them. It is more comfortable not to set goals at all than to fail at reaching those you have set.

Try setting only a few easily attainable goals; when those are reached, add more. Allow yourself the satisfaction of reaching goals you've set.

Goals are *measurable.* For instance, "staying attractive and fit" may be a hoped-for priority, but it isn't a goal because it is not specifically measurable. "Maintaining my wait at X pounds" certainly is measurable, and every morning as I step on the scales, I am immediately aware if I have wavered a pound from that ideal weight and need to adjust my diet for the day accordingly. Make your goals specific and measurable so you know when you have reached them.

Goals are *targets for the future*. That is, they stretch me beyond what I am currently achieving. From the example I used about weight, you could accuse me of not taking my own advice. However, if I don't keep that goal before me, weighing myself daily and taking appropriate action, I will repeat what I have done in the past too many times — catch the upswing of a "roller coaster" ride to a twenty-pound increase. The weight gain may come from nibbling on Christmas fruitcake, fudge, or cookies, or from making a "taste study" of the differences among Belgian, Swiss, German and Austrian chocolates as I travel.

With few exceptions, you should set goals that stretch you beyond current levels of achievement.

SETTING GOALS FOR THIS SEASON

Goals usually are set for the season of life in which you now find yourself. It would be a monumental task to establish actual goals for each season of your future, since many variables could and probably will change.

An exception to this would be if you are approaching the transition from one season to another. At that time it may be beneficial for you to look far enough ahead to establish at least a few goals within the next period, to ease the passage through the seasonal doors.

As you work at setting your seasonal goals, use your "Seasons of Life" chart from the last chapter. Then follow these guidelines:

Choose the Best Time — First, determine the approximate number of years you have remaining within the season in which you find yourself today. Look at the chart and try to plug the ambitions you wrote down for this season of life into the years you have left. Use the same principle you did in the last chapter with the "Life Focus" and "Season of Life" charts.

In the last chapter I gave the example of my Thanksgiving dinner and how I worked backward to achieve the time plan necessary to serve the dinner at the desired hour. Now we are working backward with your priorities in life to achieve a time plan to assure that you follow through with lifelong choices. You first determined what is important to accomplish within your lifetime. Then you plugged this into the various seasons of life, and now into years within a season.

If you are having trouble squeezing everything into the years of this current season, ask yourself which things could possibly be deferred to a future season, and which things could you begin now and finish later. For instance, you may begin working toward a goal of earning a college degree by taking one course each semester while you are in the "Family with Preschool Children" season. As you enter the "Family with School-age Children" season, perhaps you can handle two classes per semester, and actually finish the degree when you become an "Empty-nester."

Be Creative — You may be able to delegate, as I did with my office responsibilities and women's ministries at my church. I can accomplish those goals through other people. Be creative in your efforts to fulfill goals which are important to you.

Reevaluate Your Priorities — Again let me urge you to go before God as you study your priorities with a microscopic analysis. With what does God burden your heart? You may find that some things take on a much higher priority than other things. Don't be afraid to use an eraser. Your value as a person does not diminish if you decide that one or several of the priorities are not as important as it first appeared, and you are not willing to commit your valuable time to it.

Be true to yourself and what you want to

accomplish, remembering again that it's God who puts the desires into your heart as you go before Him seeking to please Him. Other people may try to set your priorities and goals for you, but you must determine what is most important to you, what brings you the most satisfaction when achieved, and what would most please God.

SETTING GOALS FOR THIS YEAR

Consider the unique demands on your time each year within this season. For instance, if you have children in junior high or high school, a substantial amount of your time is demanded as you taxi them to places they need to go. When they secure their own driver's license and you feel comfortable allowing them to take the car themselves, much of your time will be made available, and other goals can rise to the top of your priority list.

Consider the Necessities First — If you have preschool children, you must take time to nourish and care for them. Changing diapers, bathing babies, and wiping runny noses is time-consuming. For those years, don't set unrealistic goals which, if not completed, will cause you frustration and discouragement.

Don't Forget Yourself — Often we as Christian

women get so involved in meeting the needs of others that we forget to take time to refresh ourselves. If you have flown on a commercial airliner lately, you will recognize the speech which the flight attendants recite just before takeoff. It goes something like this, "In the event of a loss of cabin pressure, an oxygen mask will automatically be lowered. If you are sitting beside a child, first secure your own mask before applying the child's."

Why would they advise you to do that? Are they promoting an "adults over children" philosophy? Hardly. They realize that unless you as the adult are getting the oxygen you need, you'll be of no help to the child, and you will both perish.

Jesus, filled with absolute love and compassion, went to the mountains to spend time with His Father in prayer, to renew His weary body and soul. When the crowd pressed in upon Him, He suggested to the disciples that they all get away from the crowd and go to the mountains alone.

Are you getting enough "oxygen" in your life to be of maximum benefit to those around you? It is not a selfish gesture to set goals allowing you to "refill your cup." Just as an empty teakettle will crack or melt as the heat under it is turned up, so you also will break as the heat of life is turned on "high" when your "cup" — your emotional and spiritual life — is dry.

How do you refresh your soul? Set realistic goals that afford you the opportunity to do so. If you have small children, perhaps you can trade baby-sitting time with a friend or neighbor to allow each of you a morning or a day a week to meet with a friend for lunch, to visit the cosmetic counter for an update of your makeup, or to take a walk in the woods or at the beach.

Don't Forget Others — Giving to other people doesn't necessarily involve money. The gift of encouragement has immeasurable significance. My husband's high school English teacher recognized Bobb's ability and encouraged him. Without her affirmations he never would have considered college, but her few words were pivotal in the direction of his entire life.

The gift of your time to make a phone call to assure a needy friend of your prayers may be just what she needs to keep her out of depression.

"You did so well; I'm proud of you!" — those words whispered in the ear of a child after the Christmas performance may be just what is needed to make him feel a sense of approval when he is unsure of how he fared on stage.

Holding the hands of someone grieving over a lost loved one, or of someone terminally ill, is a gesture that says "I care." So often this is all that's required to sustain needy people.

The Bible tells us we are to encourage one another. Whose cheerleader are you? Be there for someone. Reach down, grab a hand, and pull someone up. You can do that no matter what stage of life you are in or how much education or money you have or don't have. You'll find yourself smiling more because you'll be happier being who you are. To fill someone else's cup will actually help you fill yours.

Consider the Seven Areas of Life — It isn't necessary to give equal weight to each of the seven areas of life within every season or year, but each area at least deserves consideration.

For example, if you're currently in the "Family with Preschool Children" season, much more of your time is devoted to the Family/Marriage area than if you are a widow or even if you have children in school. While you have babies at home, the majority of your activity in the Physical area may consist of bending over to pick up toys off the floor. (Later, aerobics may be necessary to give you the same amount of exercise.) And while you may have few goals in the Mental/Professional area in this season of life, this aspect should not be completely ignored. Do something to stimulate your mind — perhaps a college class via television, or a language learned via audio tapes. You could play language tapes while you are playing with blocks on the floor with your child. Who knows?...Perhaps your child's first word will be in French or German.

Regardless of the season in which you find yourself, if you are married, take the time to work on that relationship. The Bible tells you to leave your parents in order to transfer your highest love and loyalty to your marriage partner. It does not tell you to leave your parents and cleave to your *children*. According to God's Word, the marriage relationship is of highest importance, next to your relationship with God.

With today's divorce rate soaring even within our Christian community, I urge you to take time to cultivate and protect your marriage. A friend once said to me, "If the grass is greener on the other side of the fence, try watering the grass on your own side." Plan fun times together. If your budget is restricted, use your creativity. A fulfilling marriage requires hard work and effort but the results are disproportionately rewarding.

My personal challenge in this area is this: that

in the way I look, act, and relate to Bobb, both in and out of the bedroom, he will always be proud to introduce me as his wife. As he surveys every woman he meets, I want Bobb to be able to tell me without hesitation, "If I had it to do over again, I'd still choose you. I've got a rare diamond in my home; why should I go for a chunk of coal outside?"

You were irresistible enough to attract your spouse… now be fascinating enough to keep him. Perhaps he is a godly man and would never leave you because of biblical prohibitions, but do what you can to ensure that he never wishes he could. If your marriage is struggling today, ask your pastor or a trusted friend for help.

PUTTING IT ON CHARTS

YEARLY FOCUS

With these considerations and definitions in mind, take a look at the following "YEARLY FOCUS" chart (a sample is provided). Again, this chart applies to the years you have remaining within *this present season.*

(Before writing anything down, make copies of the blank "YEARLY FOCUS" chart for your use now and in future seasons.)

Begin completing this chart by filling in the current year at the top of the first column on the left. Continue labeling the columns to the right by listing each year remaining in this season of your life.

Now refer back at your "Seasons of Life" chart, and look again at everything listed under the first column on the left (which is this season's list). Take time to consider each goal carefully to determine (1) if it is actually worthy of your time, and (2) if it fits best into this particular year.

You may not have any goals in some of the areas of life. That is all right. Set the goals with which you are most comfortable.

Feel free to make copies of this chart for use in future years.

When to update this chart: Establish your yearly goals as you move from one season of life to another but review them at least annually to make necessary adjustments.

YEARLY FOCUS

YEAR>	*1990*	*1991*
SPIRITUAL	*Keep focused on God* *15 minutes daily personal time* *with God*	*Keep focused on God* *15 minutes daily personal time* *with God*
FAMILY/ MARRIAGE	*Give birth to child #2* *Be the best mother I can be* *Weekend away with husband once* *each quarter*	*Be the best mother I can be* *Weekend away with husband once* *each quarter*
PROFESSIONAL/ MENTAL		
PHYSICAL		*Get weight back to normal after* *pregnancy*
FINANCIAL	*Tithe to church*	*Tithe to church*
PERSONAL DEVELOPMENT		
SOCIAL/ FRIENDS	*Dinner & evening out with* *friends once a month*	*Dinner & evening out with* *friends once a month*

SEASON: *FAMILY WITH PRESCHOOL CHILDREN*

1992	1993	<YEAR
Keep focused on God 15 minutes daily personal time with God	Keep focused on God 15 minutes daily personal time with God	SPIRITUAL
Be the best mother I can be Weekend away with husband once each quarter	Give birth to child #3 Be the best mother I can be Weekend away with husband once each quarter	FAMILY/ MARRIAGE
		PROFESSIONAL/ MENTAL
		PHYSICAL
Tithe to church	Tithe to church	FINANCIAL
		PERSONAL DEVELOPMENT
Dinner & evening out with friends once a month	Dinner & evening out with friends once a month	SOCIAL/ FRIENDS

YEARLY FOCUS

YEAR>		
SPIRITUAL		
FAMILY/ MARRIAGE		
PROFESSIONAL/ MENTAL		
PHYSICAL		
FINANCIAL		
PERSONAL DEVELOPMENT		
SOCIAL/ FRIENDS		

SEASON:

		<YEAR
		SPIRITUAL
		FAMILY/ MARRIAGE
		PROFESSIONAL/ MENTAL
		PHYSICAL
		FINANCIAL
		PERSONAL DEVELOPMENT
		SOCIAL/ FRIENDS

Quarterly Focus

Using the same principles, carefully determine which of the yearly goals you would like to begin, work on, or actually complete this quarter. *(Before writing anything down, make copies of the blank "QUARTERLY FOCUS" chart for your use now and in future quarters.)* On your "Quarterly Focus" chart for this quarter, fill in the remaining months of the current quarter. (See the sample.)

Again, be realistic; don't overcommit yourself. Take into consideration seasonal holidays, vacations you plan to take, and guests who are planning to visit — all of these will require extra amounts of your time. There may be time blocks when you will be away and cannot satisfy routine goals.

For instance, during the last quarter of the year, most women are very busy preparing special meals for Thanksgiving, Christmas, and New Year's, besides shopping and decorating for these holidays. So it probably isn't a wise plan to remodel your home during that quarter, but it may be a perfect time to fulfill social goals by having a holiday party.

The quarterly focus simply answers the question, **"If I am to accomplish my yearly**

goals, which of them should I plan on reaching during this particular quarter?"

When to update: Establish your quarterly goals one year at a time, just before the year begins. Then review and rework them each quarter just before the quarter begins.

QUARTERLY FOCUS

QUARTER>	*January–March*	*April–June*
SPIRITUAL	*Keep focused on God* *15 minutes daily personal time* *with God*	*Keep focused on God* *15 minutes daily personal time* *with God*
FAMILY/ MARRIAGE	*Prepare #1 child for #2's birth* *Weekend away with husband*	*Prepare #1 child for #2's birth* *Weekend away with husband*
PROFESSIONAL/ MENTAL		
PHYSICAL		
FINANCIAL	*Tithe to church* *Save for baby expenses*	*Tithe to church* *Save for baby expenses*
PERSONAL DEVELOPMENT		
SOCIAL/ FRIENDS	*Dinner & evening out with* *friends once a month*	*Dinner & evening out with* *friends once a month*

YEAR: *1990*

July–September	*October–December*	<QUARTER
Keep focused on God 15 minutes daily personal time with God	Keep focused on God 15 minutes daily personal time with God	SPIRITUAL
Give birth to child #2	Adjust to having 2 children	FAMILY/ MARRIAGE
		PROFESSIONAL/ MENTAL
	Begin exercise to get weight back to normal	PHYSICAL
Tithe to church Added baby expenses	Tithe to church Added baby expenses	FINANCIAL
		PERSONAL DEVELOPMENT
Dinner & evening out with friends once a month	Dinner & evening out with friends once a month	SOCIAL/ FRIENDS

QUARTERLY FOCUS

QUARTER>		
SPIRITUAL		
FAMILY/ MARRIAGE		
PROFESSIONAL/ MENTAL		
PHYSICAL		
FINANCIAL		
PERSONAL DEVELOPMENT		
SOCIAL/ FRIENDS		

YEAR:

		<QUARTER
		SPIRITUAL
		FAMILY/ MARRIAGE
		PROFESSIONAL/ MENTAL
		PHYSICAL
		FINANCIAL
		PERSONAL DEVELOPMENT
		SOCIAL/ FRIENDS

WEEKLY FOCUS

If the "Quarterly Focus" chart helps you determine which yearly goals are accomplished this quarter, the "WEEKLY FOCUS" chart answers the question, "**If I am to accomplish my quarterly goals, which of them should I focus on this particular week?**" If you want to accomplish your quarterly goals, take each goal and plug it into a week. You will need three of these charts, one for each month of the quarter.

(Before writing anything down, make copies of the blank "Weekly Focus" chart for your use now and in the future.)

If you cannot find the time for a particular goal, then reconsider the value of it or other goals which may be preventing you from accomplishing that one. Review the "good" and "best" values. At each step of sifting goals through the tunnel of time, continue this reevaluation process: *Is this goal worthy of my time? Is this a "best," or is it a "good" robbing me of a "best"?* Consider the amount of time each goal will take. Are you willing to give this project or person that much of yourself, or is there something or someone else that deserves higher priority?

Establishing your weekly focus is NOT equivalent to setting a weekly "to do" list. Rather, it means establishing what the *focus* of the week will be. For the week of Thanksgiving, my weekly focus is simply "Thanksgiving dinner." The focus of the week before Christmas might be "Finish Christmas shopping."

When to update: Establish your weekly focus one quarter at a time, just before the quarter begins. Then review each week's list just before the week begins.

WEEKLY FOCUS

WEEK>	Dec. 29—Jan. 6	Jan. 7—13
SPIRITUAL	15 minutes daily personal time with God	15 minutes daily personal time with God
FAMILY/ MARRIAGE	Make trip plans for weekend away	Arrange babysitting for weekend away
PROFESSIONAL/ MENTAL		
PHYSICAL		
FINANCIAL		$50 savings for baby expenses
PERSONAL DEVELOPMENT		
SOCIAL/ FRIENDS		

MONTH: *JANUARY 1990*

Jan. 14—20	*Jan. 21—27*	*Jan. 28—Feb.3*
15 minutes daily personal time with God	15 minutes daily personal time with God	15 minutes daily personal time with God
Weekend away with husband		Buy bigger bed for child #1
	$50 savings for baby expenses	Pay for new bed
Invite friends to dinner & evening out	Make arrangements for dinner reservations, babysitter	Dinner & evening out with friends

WEEKLY FOCUS

WEEK>		
SPIRITUAL		
FAMILY/ MARRIAGE		
PROFESSIONAL/ MENTAL		
PHYSICAL		
FINANCIAL		
PERSONAL DEVELOPMENT		
SOCIAL/ FRIENDS		

MONTH:

DAILY FOCUS

The same goal-setting procedure continues for establishing your "DAILY FOCUS." Again, I'm not talking about a daily "to do" list, but rather a general focus for each day. It may be "cleaning," "laundry," or "rest." If you are a career woman, perhaps your daily focus might be "studying reports from last month's general ledger," or "reviewing the Jones account."

Establishing a daily focus isn't deciding every detail of your day; rather, it means plugging in the *overall theme* of the day. It eliminates the "What shall I do today?" question that often consumes a block of time as we seem to tread water trying to establish the best use of our time for that day. When the week's work seems like an insurmountable mountain, break it into workable days. This will reduce that mountain into climbable molehills.

When to update: Establish your daily focus one week at a time, just before your week begins, Then review it the next day, the night before.

(I haven't included a "Daily Focus" chart in this chapter; instead it is presented in the next chapter as part of a complete notebook system.)

A Taxing Example

The principle behind this book — define each task and break it down into workable units — applies to many areas of life. I encourage you to examine necessary tasks that you tend not to enjoy, and see if applying this principle affords some relief to you. That's exactly what I have experienced.

One of my most unpleasant and dreaded annual responsibilities is preparing our taxes. Several years ago, when I was encouraged by our financial advisor to assume this responsibility, I examined it from all angles, studied the various aspects of it, and went about accepting the challenge of learning the details of tax accounting. But as someone of gregarious persuasion, I love working with people much more; it takes sheer discipline for me to sit behind a desk and work with numbers and forms. In other words, I hate to do taxes!

To me, taxes are a Mount Everest I have to climb once a year. Until they're completed, every minute between January 1 and April 15 that I'm not working on taxes finds me so oppressed by guilt that I'm robbed of any pleasure I would normally find in pursuing social endeavors.

This has been a particularly busy year for me, and it was near the end of March before I even looked at the general ledger to begin compiling numbers for Uncle Sam. When I could procrastinate no longer, I spread out the necessary documents on my desk and surveyed the forms to be completed — fifteen in total.

As I stared at the blank forms, I realized that the overwhelming nature of the problem at hand had kept me from seeing the solution. Suddenly it dawned on me: The individual forms were the workable units into which the mountain of taxes could be broken. Completing one form each day would comfortably allow me to finish the task in fifteen days. No sweat! One form a day was easy. I was almost looking forward to doing it — at least I was looking forward to having the job done.

I had taken the long, dark tunnel — the light at the end of which I could not see — and cut it into fifteen small tunnels, each of which had a bright and clearly visible light at the end.

Each day after I completed only one form, I felt a sense of accomplishment. I had fulfilled my plan for that day and wasn't burdened by not having completed the entire project. My one heavy load turned into fifteen light chores, and in two weeks the job was completed.

I had a satisfied smile on my face; this year our taxes had been a "piece of cake."

DISCUSSION QUESTIONS:

1. Whose cheerleader are you? Who is your
    cheerleader? Does any single person
    stand out in your life as your personal
    encourager?

2. What are you doing at this point in your
    life to get "oxygen" for yourself so you can
    in turn meet other people's needs?

3. If you could only do one thing in your life, what would it be? How can you use your creativity to realize that dream? (Brain-storm in your discussion group to expand your thinking in this area.)

4. Have goals ever represented failure to you? When did they represent success?

5. What are you feeling overwhelmed by that you could break down into workable units and experience progress in as you complete steps along the way?

4

Living with a Notebook

IF YOU BLINDFOLDED my father-in-law, twirled him around until he was dizzy, led him through a deep and unfamiliar woods, and asked him at high noon with the sun straight overhead which way was north, his arm would stretch out and point as accurately north as a compass needle. He doesn't need a compass... *I* need a compass.

I remember my mother showing me how to make pie crust. She said she added flour and carefully mixed it with her hands until it "feels right." She doesn't need a recipe. *I* need a recipe.

If you need to have the dentist send you a reminder in the mail that six months have passed since your last visit and it's time for another one, or you can't remember each of your friend's birthdays to whom you really want to send a card, or you sometimes forget when to fertilize which plants with what food, or when to take the car in for servicing, or when your husband's flight arrives at which airport on which airline and what flight number, or when your child had his last tetanus shot, or what your husband's social security number is, or what blood types each of your children has — then you need a notebook system... just as *I* need a notebook system.

The truth is, in today's society our lives are not simple. Our brains are overloaded with details. I know *I* need help. And since you chose to read this book, I'm assuming you do too.

Not everyone needs or can use the same notebook system. To a large extent your responsibilities in life at this particular time determine your needs. Generally speaking, the more details or activities for which you are responsible, the more systematized, organized, and detailed your notebook needs to be.

If you're the mother of one toddler and have a housekeeper and a gardener, you may need only a place to keep a shopping list, a name and address system, and a small calendar. On the other hand, if you have five children ranging in age from five to seventeen and you are the PTA chairwoman, head of the annual bazaar at church, and teacher of a Sunday School class, you need a notebook with several tabs to keep track of the many details for which you are responsible.

Your personality type is another variable in determining the type of notebook to best suit your needs. My husband developed an inventory he calls the "Role Preference Inventory." He explains that every project goes through several phases: the design phase, then the development of that design, and lastly the management of the project.

As the project develops, one's personality type will largely determine which stage of the project he or she enjoys most. For instance, some people like to sit down with a blank piece of paper and create an idea for a project that they have never seen before. Other people don't have original ideas but like to take other people's ideas and develop them into a completed project. The people who design the project may be absolutely lost when it comes to making it happen, whereas the people who thrive on developing it might stare at the wall for hours if asked to come up with an original design.

Then there are some people who love to *maintain* the details of a project, refining it until they have a more effective, smoothly running system. Again, these people might have no idea how to develop it and even less of an idea of how to originate it. Meanwhile the originators and the developers of the project might well be absolutely bored with the thought of maintaining it.

So within each of these three project phases are places where people find their niche.

Do you know someone whose house is always a mess but she doesn't care if children are there with crayons or fingerpaints in hand drawing pictures? That person is probably a designer and sees no real value in a spotless house, but places tremendous worth on freedom of expression.

If you're this type of person, you may see little value in embracing the totality of the notebook I'm about to explain. I would suggest that you take from these pages what will *help* you. I have no interest in making you feel guilty or saying you "should" complete each and every section.

On the other hand, if you enjoy developing or maintaining a project, you will appreciate the value of a notebook; moreover, the more details the notebook offers, the more you will embrace and use its features.

If you have been counting on your memory to keep track of your life and it isn't working, or if you write things down on little pieces of paper and find them weeks later in the pocket of a sweater, perhaps some sort of a notebook will help you. Use whatever helps you achieve the things you have decided are important to you.

It's critical to know and accept your own personality. Don't despise yourself for who you are, and don't despise someone else for being different from you. Be the person God made you to be. In 1 Peter 4:10-11 we read that each of us is given different gifts to be used within the body of Christ.

The system I'm about to explain to you is one that works for me. It's my compass, my road map. I affectionately refer to it as my brain. If I use it, my dreams become realities. I'm able to say "yes" to what I have carefully chosen as my priorities and goals, and "no" to things of lower priority. Many excellent systems are available to help you achieve organization in your life. I'm not trying to impose this one on you, but I will share it with you because it works for me.

The notebook is divided into three sections:

FOCUS and CALENDAR

PEOPLE and PROJECTS
for Which I'm Responsible

DETAILS I Need to Keep Track Of

1. FOCUS AND CALENDAR

THE FIRST THREE CHAPTERS of this book have dealt with setting one's focus, which I believe is most important. The rest of the book is simply a suggested strategy for implementing your carefully selected focus. You already have spent a lot of time determining what you consider most important as you sorted through the thousands of options before you, and as you thought about your strengths and needs according to what God has shown you.

You have considered what you would like to accomplish during your lifetime, and have put those priorities into the present and future seasons of your life. Within the season in which you currently find yourself, you have plotted priorities across the years. And then, for *this* year, you've decided what you will aim to accomplish. Narrowing it even further, you decided what you might accomplish this quarter and each week within this quarter. Lastly, you've begun to name a focus for each day of this week.

Having produced that skeleton, let's do some serious thinking about the muscles, ligaments, tendons, organs, and skin you'll want to put on those bones. What do you actually want to do each day? Again, I would urge you first and most

importantly to go before our Lord to regain a
clear understanding of who He is, who you are
(your limitations and strengths) and where He
would have you commit your time.

Several years ago, when Bobb worked at
World Vision International, we were close friends
of his colleague, Bill Needham, and his wife,
Jean. Bill's responsibilities included presenting to
the president a daily summary of world events
that pertained to World Vision. Bill did outstanding work; he never seemed in a hurry, never
appeared overwhelmed, and always seemed to be
in control. When Bobb inquired about his secret,
Bill gave the following analogy.

He said he thought of his schedule as an egg
basket, and his activities and responsibilities as
the eggs. Since an egg basket will hold only a
given number of eggs, there comes a point at
which a new egg introduced to the basket will
either fall, crashing to the floor, or cause another
one to be the "Humpty Dumpty."

Bill then explained that when the president
asked him to take on another responsibility, he
would respond by saying he would be happy to
do that, but his schedule (egg basket) was
presently full. Then he would ask the president
which of his other responsibilities (eggs) he

should postpone, delegate, or ignore in order to complete this new one.

I'll take the analogy one step further. At various seasons in our lives our egg baskets are of different sizes or shapes. They accommodate different numbers or sizes of eggs. Sometimes one or two eggs are disproportionately heavy. Even though the basket looks rather empty to other people, adding even one more small egg would make it impossible for the owner to carry. Only *you* can determine which eggs and how many are appropriate and comfortable for your basket.

Try to organize each week before it begins. Get as many details in on Saturday or Sunday night as you can. You already have established the focus for the week and for each day. Now is the time to finalize the particulars.

Start with the non-negotiables. These could be your children's athletic games, parent-teacher conferences, and other events or appointments at which you need to appear but have no control over the appointed time.

Second, plug in the things you must do and over which you do control the time or day. Dental appointments and grocery shopping are examples. You may decide to designate one day per week for such appointments or errands in order to keep every day from seeming to be chopped up into bits and pieces.

After you have scheduled the non-negotiable items, pull out your focus charts to see what else you may have time to do today. What did you put on your weekly focus chart that fits the time block available to you today? If this is your day for errands, you may not have any time available. Move on to the next day, and evaluate the time available.

PRINCIPLES TO REMEMBER

Guard Your Calendar Carefully. Your calendar represents where you will spend your precious, limited time. Because you are given a fixed amount of time on this earth, it's up to you to determine where and how you will spend it. If you allow other people to impose their priorities on your time, you will eventually resent those people and feel robbed because your own goals are not met.

You've already asked God to make clear to you what is the best use of your time, and you've established significant goals. Now do what you need to do to have time for realizing those priorities and goals.

Some of you reading this book will find this organized approach to be freeing, relieving your fears of forgetting something important or not getting everything done. Others will find it confining and inhibiting to your spontaneity. I would suggest that you read and carefully consider all of the options. Then choose what best meets your needs. Remember, you are human and not a machine. YOU CAN'T DO EVERY-THING. Give yourself permission not to be perfect.

You Don't Have Time to Waste. Learn the distinctions between rest, play, and waste. God commands us to get rest for our bodies. We actually accomplish more if we take time to rest and relax than if we work our body continuously without rest. If you're tired, it is not a waste of time to take a nap.

Within each of us lives a child, no matter what our age. I love roller coasters, slides, swings, and Disneyland. I stand (I should say *swim*) in awe of God's creation as I scuba dive. A goal on my next year's calendar is to learn to parachute. I've been told the exhilaration of the free fall is beyond description. This type of diversion from the intensity we experience as we stretch toward reaching our goals is play, and it's necessary.

However, none of us has time to waste. According to Webster, to *waste* means "to use up or spend without real need, gain, or purpose; squander; to wear away; consume gradually; use up." To rest has a purpose. To play has a purpose. To waste has no purpose or value.

What is considered play or rest for one person may actually be wasteful for another. For example, when my head hits the pillow, an internal switch clicks off. I can drink fifteen cups of coffee and still fall directly asleep when I put my body in that horizontal position. My husband, however, seems to carry his thoughts to bed, and the proverbial wheels of his brain continue to turn. The most effective way for him to coerce those wheels to a halt is to watch a detective show on television.

For Bobb to watch that show under those circumstances is actually a necessity to get the rest he needs. But for me to watch such a program by myself is a waste, because I neither enjoy it nor does it serve any purpose or meet any need. To watch it with Bobb, however, is a chance to hold his hand and spend time with him. That changes it from a waste to a priority.

TIME-SAVING TIPS

Learn the art of accomplishing more than one thing at a time. For example, keep a book you want to read in your car. As you sit in the doctor's waiting room with a sick child, don't find yourself with no reading options other than the magazines subscribed to by the receptionist. Get the book from your car, and read what you *choose* to read.

Or, if the child isn't too sick, use this time to talk with him or her to catch up on necessary news or to explore new ideas. Use the time to discuss and listen, not lecture.

Also keep in your car any tapes you may have listed in the "Personal Development" column of your charts. As you drive down the freeway, listen to these tapes rather than a radio program that may be of no value or interest to you.

Practice time-saving tips to take full advantage of precious hours in your day. For instance, while you are talking on the phone is a good time to be doing two things at once. Plan ahead of time some "brainless," routine tasks that, if planned for, can be completed during this time. For instance, I use this time to take a favorite rose or border stamp and decorate plain

scrap paper left over from business printings —
it's instantly transformed into stationery notes.
Doing this doesn't require my thinking, so I am
not distracted from the conversation.

A friend of mine keeps magazines near the
phone and browses through them, dog-earring
pages of articles she would like to read when she
is waiting at the doctor's office, or in the car for
her son to finish up his soccer practice.

Another friend has a business of making and
painting wooden necklaces. When she budgets
time to paint, she also catches up on her phone
calls and keeps in contact with friends.

Having a portable phone gives even more
flexibility for accomplishing such things as
making the bed or doing laundry while talking
on the phone.

The principle is simple: Combine things that
require thinking with things that don't, or things
that require your presence (flying in an airplane)
with things that require your attention (cross-
stitching). Make a list of things you might be able
to do during otherwise unoccupied time.

Another time-saver: When you are cooking,
double the recipe and freeze the part you don't
use for a later time. Several years ago, when I was

not working and did a lot of entertaining, I relied heavily on a particular recipe book that was designed for the gourmet cook who wished to freeze a partially cooked meal. On many occasions I would spend three days preparing dinners for two weeks. The first day was spent planning the menus, the second in making a grocery list and purchasing the ingredients, and the third day I spent in the kitchen preparing the meals.

As the sauce for the lasagna simmered for five hours, I would cook rice and sauté the scallions for stuffed cabbage leaves. While the scallions were sautéing, I grated cheese for the next entrée. By the end of the day my freezer was full. When guests and relatives were here for a prolonged visit, as we left for Disneyland in the morning I would put the frozen dinner in the oven with a timer set, so that as we walked in the door that evening, dinner was ready.

Setting up a simple filing system can give you a disproportionate return for your time invested. A very simple example from my own life is is a system I set up for greeting cards. When I have a few extra moments while shopping, I sometimes browse in the stationery store. If I happen to see a few cards that appeal to me, I purchase them. I have set up a hanging-file system for different groupings of cards: "Friendship," "Birthday," "Get Well," "Anniversary," and so on.

It took me perhaps thirty minutes to set up that system. When I return home after purchasing cards, it takes me no more than three minutes to file the new cards I have acquired. Later, if I hear of a friend's illness, it takes me all of about thirty seconds to find a suitable card to send.

If I had to sort through an unorganized box of cards I had collected, it might take me thirty minutes to find the ideal choice; and if I had to go to the store for each occasion, my friends might never get cards. That one half hour I spent setting up this system has saved me many hours of time and frustration through the years, and it has kept me in close contact with my friends.

Another system not only saves time, but also helps assure that you won't forget to pay bills or send important documents on time. This "tickler" system can be maintained by keeping a plastic see-through folder by the phone or in another highly visible location at home. Inside the folder are envelopes (such as those containing payment for bills) which are sorted by due date, ready to send. The next to be mailed is in front. When a bill comes in the mail, put the date to be sent where the stamp will go and file it in the plastic folder. Since you see the file daily you will not likely overlook mailing these important envelopes.

Another filing system I've greatly benefitted from is a travel system. When I read a magazine article about an interesting place I'd like to visit, I tear out the article and file it in a folder bearing the name of that city or country. When I plan our next trip, I don't have to spend time searching for the article. Interesting information on the particular country or city we wish to visit is at my fingertips in one handy folder.

There are countless time-saving tips to use as you learn to plan ahead. When a friend plans her calendar a month in advance, she calls her favorite baby-sitter and arranges for her to sit on those particular nights when she will be out. Since very few women are so organized, she has top priority with her choice of sitters. It also saves her time to make one call for the month rather than one call per evening out.

Learn to make and save lists that you can use repeatedly — articles to pack for camping trips, places to go when out of town guests visit, information for baby sitters, directions to infrequently visited places, and so on. If you have a computer, you may want to store this information there rather than carrying it with you in your notebook.

DON'T LET THE GOOD ROB YOU OF THE BEST. You've heard this principle before, but "goods" knock on the daily calendar frequently and are often more easily allowed in the door than they would be on the yearly, seasonal, or lifetime charts. When you establish your seasonal goals, you will not allow a "good" to waste a year of your life, but when you view a day, you rationalize: "It's only one day. What does that matter in a lifetime?" That's valid reasoning if it is *just* one day, but it's too easy for this to happen consistently; before we realize it, a week has passed. We look back in disappointment because we have accomplished nothing of significant value. A week of our life has been wasted.

If you allow this to happen, don't think being organized is hopeless, and therefore abandon the idea. Instead, try to reestablish the procedures and goals. One day or a week off the schedule doesn't mean total failure. Priorities and goals need to be reevaluated, and then you can return to your notebook organization. Old habits are hard to break, but the efforts put forth to accomplish change promise inestimable benefits.

Having your calendar already scheduled with what is "best" for you allows an easier "no" to a request for a "good." If you only vaguely plan to do a "best" sometime this week, when a request for a "good" comes along you may be pressured into accepting it because of an open spot in your calendar. That may keep you from accomplishing your "best."

An example of this might be a desire to visit your neighbor who is in the hospital. You believe this is a "best," but have not yet scheduled it on your calendar. Let's suppose another friend calls and asks you to ride with her to pick up her mail order which has just arrived at a store some distance away. Since nothing is on your calendar at the moment, you agree to go and don't return for two hours. As you study your week that evening, you see that the only time you could have visited your neighbor this week was that day. The "good" robbed you of the "best."

On the other side of the coin, perhaps the friend who called wanting you to ride with her is having marital problems and needs your listening ear and counsel. Riding with her may be the very best use of your time for that day. Conceivably, a phone call to your hospitalized friend may be sufficient. When an opportunity arises, evaluate its importance for your day, and be willing to be flexible with your schedule in order to accommodate unforeseen opportunities — which may even be better than what you originally perceived to be the best for that day.

Another situation which demands your flexibility is sickness. If your child or husband is ill, other things need to go on hold. Consider scheduling one afternoon for catching up with what simply didn't get done as scheduled. Don't pack your calendar so full that you have no room for flexibility.

The particular notebook system I use is called "Day-Focus." The focus and calendar tabs are found horizontally across the top of the pages.

On the next page is a copy of the daily calendar taken from the Day-Focus system. I particularly like this design with the times listed on the left half of the page, and the sections "Day-Focus," "To Do Today," "To Write," "Phone" and "Misc/Expenses" on the right side. There's also a place to number the priorities for the day and a spot to check them off when completed. The bottom of the page is focused on the family needs. Again, this system's design meets my individual needs, but if it doesn't meet yours, find or design one that does.

APPOINTMENTS & SCHEDULED EVENTS	#	✓	DAY FOCUS
5 05:00		●	
6 06:00			TO DO TODAY
7 07:00			
8 08:00			
9 09:00			
10 10:00			
11 11:00			TO WRITE/DICTATE
12 12:00			
1 13:00			
2 14:00			PHONE
3 15:00			
4 16:00			
5 17:00			
6 18:00			
7 19:00			MISC./EXPENSES
8 20:00			
9 21:00			

PERSONAL/FAMILY FOCUS/HOME

DAY FOCUS	#	✓	TO WRITE/PHONE	CALENDAR
●				
●				
●				
TO DO TODAY			FITNESS/MISC.	

PUT ON YOUR CHRISTMAS MUSIC AND LET'S PLAN YOUR CALENDAR

Someone quoted an "expert" who claimed that women spend more time planning Christmas than they do the rest of their lives. Perhaps that is true of you, or perhaps Christmas is one of those seasons in which you find yourself harried and frazzled, never seeming to get everything finished. By planning Christmas ahead of time, you'll be able to focus on Jesus, the real meaning of Christmas. The season will become more enjoyable as you take control of the details. You don't have to be a "wonder woman" to accomplish everything you most want to do or that is your best choice.

To demonstrate how this system can work practically, I'd like to propose a generic Christmas countdown. Please revise it for your own use if it's helpful to you. Get out your calendar, put on a Christmas tape, and start adding your details into my suggestions.

Let's begin with a partial list of quarterly goals:

October — December
Serve Thanksgiving dinner
Attend husband's office party
Shop for Christmas gifts

Purchase and send Christmas cards
Decorate home
Serve Christmas dinner to family

Now let's move to the week of Thanksgiving and look at our weekly goals:

week of November 20:
Thanksgiving dinner
Decorate for Christmas

week of November 27:
Make Christmas lists
Buy Christmas cards

week of December 4:
Send Christmas cards
Begin gift shopping

week of December 11:
Finish gift shopping
Organize Christmas dinner

week of December 18:
Shop for Christmas dinner
Attend office party

week of December 25:
Merry Christmas!
Serve Christmas dinner

Now for the daily schedule. Of course, I am only putting in the Christmas plans here, and not taking into account the other responsibilities that you have. The final time balances are critical at this point. Don't over-schedule yourself in any one day. Try to distribute things equally enough that no single day carries a disproportionate amount of the load.

Let's pick up the schedule the day after Thanksgiving:

November 24	*Decorate the house for Christmas*
	Buy poinsettias
November 25	*Plant poinsettias and finish decorating*
November 26	*REST*
November 27	*Compile children's lists*
November 28	*Compile husband's and my lists*
November 29	*Collect lists from relatives*
November 30	*Purchase Christmas cards and stamps*
November 31	*Mark address lists for cards sent*
December 1	*Make lists of friends to be given gifts and lists of gifts.*
	Make lists of shopping areas and which gifts to purchase where
December 2	*Start addressing cards*
December 3	*REST*
December 4	*Address more cards*
December 5	*Finish addressing cards, and mail them*

December 6	*Order gifts from catalogues*
December 7	*Shop at wholesale membership club*
December 8	*Shop at local mall*
December 9	*Shop at swap meet*
December 10	*REST*
December 11	*Finish gift shopping — specialty shops — misc.*
December 12	*Wrap presents and put under Christmas tree*
December 13	*Organize Christmas dinner menu*
December 14	*Make grocery list for Christmas dinner*
December 15	*Catch up on anything that didn't get done.*
December 16	*Take the kids Christmas shopping*
December 17	*REST*
December 18	*Catch up on details missed; meet friends for lunch.*
December 19	*Relax! Do non-Christmas projects.*
December 20	*Free time*
December 21	*Shop for Christmas dinner*
December 22	*Attend Christmas party*
December 23	*Get stockings ready*
December 24	*REST*
December 25	*Merry Christmas! Gifts are opened! Dinner is served!*

If you allowed the shopping and other activities to be delayed until the last minute, then once again you would feel considerable pressure. By using this planning system to break down the tasks into workable units, no single day becomes overwhelming. In fact, several days are planned that have nothing to do with Christmas.

These principles can be expanded to include making Christmas gifts throughout the year; your first quarter list, for example, might include something such as "Making an afghan for Susie."

2. PEOPLE AND PROJECTS FOR WHICH I'M RESPONSIBLE

IN THIS SECTION of your notebook, the tab headings will vary a great deal with individual situations. (Again, using the Day-Focus system, the tabs for the people and projects are found vertically on the right edge of the pages.) Let me name a few headings which might apply to you.

"Family and Marriage" will probably be a tab heading you'll include. This list may include entertainment ideas, places to visit, or amusement parks you all enjoy. It also might include an ongoing list of gifts which you hear members of the family mention they would enjoy.

Write these down so you won't forget them when Christmas or a birthday approaches.

If you're a room mother, another tab might read "Susie's classroom." Perhaps it includes a list of all students in her class, plus their parents' first names and telephone numbers. It might include dates of class field trips and lists of mothers who are willing to accompany you or to make a dessert.

One tab heading that is always appropriate is "Notes and Ideas." It's simply a place to write down an idea or take notes on an interesting speaker. Other appropriate tabs would be "Sermon Notes" and "Bible Study Class Notes."

My husband travels extensively, but he faithfully calls home each evening. I have a tab labeled "BOBBY" (as I affectionately call him), and there I write anything of either a personal or business nature that we need to speak about. Upon discussing it, I write down the appropriate action necessary. When the action is completed, I check it off the list.

I also include issues we need to discuss at length, or decisions to be made. As we have blocks of unscheduled time while driving in the car or flying together, I open my notebook to this section to jog my memory of topics to address. Perhaps you could use such a section in your notebook.

These tab headings should custom-fit your needs. This notebook is to help *you*. Make it fit exactly what you need...no more, but no less. If at this point in life you are responsible only for yourself and your children, perhaps you don't need all those divisions. You may need others which I haven't mentioned.

3. DETAILS I NEED TO KEEP TRACK OF

MOST OF US, I believe, need a place to keep track of details. However, *what* we need to keep track of certainly varies with each individual. So again, customize this last section of the notebook to fit your own needs.

Below are listed some details found in my personal notebook. In the Day-Focus system, these tabs are found horizontally across the bottoms of the pages.

PERSONAL AND MEDICAL INFORMATION

I strongly urge each of you to systemize personal and medical data. Having this particular information at my fingertips saves me literally hundreds of hours that would otherwise be spent searching for information.

Each member of my family has a separate sheet of paper. On it I include information such as:

> birthdate
> driver's license number
> Social Security number
> blood type
> life insurance policy numbers
> medical insurance policy numbers
> auto insurance policy numbers
> clothing sizes
> passport number
> allergies
> immunization record
> checking account number
> safe deposit box number
> airline frequent flyer numbers

Keeping a record of immunizations saves you trips or phone calls to the doctor, since you will need this information when the children begin or change schools, or in case of an accident. If any special medical problems occur in your family, a list of doctors with their phone numbers and a record of past treatment is invaluable.

FINANCIAL

If you adhere to a budget, your expenditures are logged here. A simple ledger sheet, kept current, saves you considerable time as you total numbers at the end of the month or quarter after the facts are cold.

Keeping track of tax-deductible items in this section is beneficial. Recording such expenditures as medical payments, contributions, interest payments, and miscellaneous deductible taxes as they are incurred will save you many hours at the end of the year. Simply totaling columns in this itemized ledger keeps you from reviewing each separate checkbook register in search of allowable deductions at tax time.

SHOPPING

If you don't need a grocery list, you are truly amazing! Keep a current list, updating it as you run out of items. Then add to that list as you plan menus.

You may also wish to keep a separate list of miscellaneous items that you need to purchase, items not available at the grocery store — for example, birthday cards and gifts. Keeping a list prevents frustration and the lingering thought that something of extreme importance has been forgotten.

Phone Lists

There are several ways to list phone numbers. You may wish to keep separate lists for family, business, and friends. Smaller and more specific groupings may also be kept. For instance, I have a tab labeled "WOMEN'S MINISTRIES," with a phone list of the "Wonder Women" I mentioned in a previous chapter. I have another one for our Growth Group. It's easy to look up the group where all the numbers are listed, rather than hunting for the numbers in a larger group of names listed alphabetically.

I used the "Record Plate" system for almost fifteen years. A strength of that system is found in the name and address setup. In a multi-ring notebook are kept separate sheets of paper full of information about each person or family you wish to include. This information would include, for instance, directions to their home, foods they especially like or dislike, birthdays of family members, correspondence, gifts exchanged, and so on.

I laud the advantage of that system, but its

bulkiness made carrying it as part of my notebook impractical. However, I've kept and stored my "Record Plate" information sheets and refer to them often.

Again, use the system which meets your needs most effectively.

"To Do" List

Keep a list of things that have no set time deadline but which need to be done whenever convenient or possible. These are things you don't want to forget and will get to as soon as you can. If you have an extra hour, look at the list; see if you can start anything, and work on it in that time frame.

This list is never completed because you are always adding to it. Don't let it be a source of frustration, but rather a help in remembering these important details. Think of your notebook (as I do) as your "brain."

Special Dates to Remember

To our embarrassment, we often forget dates we desperately want to remember every year as details overload our brain. These dates include

SPECIAL DATES TO REMEMBER

JANUARY

FEBRUARY

MARCH

APRIL

MAY

JUNE

Day-Focus™ Form: 4-0-08-689

birthdays, anniversaries of special friends, and special memories to celebrate. On the facing page you'll find a sample from the Day-Focus system of a page designed to record these special times.

This page is also effective for keeping track of seasonal dates to remember related to household or yard maintenance, such as when to fertilize certain plants or spray for insects, when to change the furnace filter, or when to turn over the mattress. Anything you need to remember to do at the same time each year can be recorded on this page.

<u>KEEP CONTROL!</u>

I remember in college a professor discussing the use of a budget. She advised, "Don't let a budget control you; you control your budget. Make it work for you."

I offer the same advice to you in regard to your notebook. Don't let it control you; you control it. Don't let it be just one more thing you need to keep track of. Let it help you maintain control of your life. If your notebook isn't working for you, change it until it does. Make it fully yours to meet your individual needs.

Be prepared to adjust your notebook as you

use it. Chances are you have rearranged your kitchen cupboards more than once since you moved into your current home or apartment. As you worked in your kitchen you realized that another configuration would save you steps or be more convenient. Just so, as you work with your notebook, make changes that make your life easier.

There are many personal notebook and time-management systems available at office supply, stationery, or specialty stores. If your own current system doesn't have everything, draw from other systems. If needed, hole-punch pages from other systems to fit yours, or make up your own pages. Design a system that maximizes your abilities and efforts to reach your carefully chosen goals.

The Day-Focus daily calendar sheet and the
Day-Focus "Special Dates to Remember" sheet
are reproduced in this chapter by permission of:

DAY-FOCUS, Inc.
31921 Camino Capistrano, Suite 9104
San Juan Capistrano, California 92675

For more information about the Day-Focus System,
write to the address above, or call 1-800-662-5300

DISCUSSION QUESTIONS:

1. Are you currently using a notebook system? Are you happy with it? What do you like best about it?

2. What details that you need to keep track of would be better maintained if they were included in your notebook? If you tend to write things on scraps of paper and then lose the scraps, what notebook categories or tab headings do you think would best help you organize those details?

CONCLUSION

Plenty of Time

It's true...

YOU CAN'T DO EVERYTHING

...but you *can* do what is best for YOU.

It may take you many hours or even several days to consider carefully the choices available to you, and to make wise decisions concerning your time commitments. But the time you spend creating a future plan pales by comparison to the time you could waste without such a design. Take the time necessary to ensure that your choices are the best. I hope this book is helping you sort out what you *can* do...what is BEST and most important for you.

Even after you've established a strategy, it's easy to get out of balance. Give yourself enough

room and flexibility to accommodate unfore-
seeable circumstances. If your child gets sick, or a
temporary volunteer position you're filling takes
an unexpected amount of time, you'll find your
"to do" list backed up. To keep on target in
reaching your goals, simply refocus as quickly as
possible.

When we returned home from Europe with
my parents, I didn't need to revise my lifetime
goals, for they hadn't changed. I didn't need to
revise my annual goals; these also hadn't
changed. But I *did* rework and revise my quarterly
priorities and then my weekly and daily goals.
Within a few hours, I had refocused; I was back
on target to reach my aspirations. It was a revised
plan, and it worked. I completed this book and all
my other "to do's" from my list of forty-three.

You can do the same.

Make annual, quarterly, and weekly adjustments. Even if nothing unforeseen gets you off
track, your priorities may change as new
challenges come your way or situations change.
Be flexible. Maintain your daily focus as you
meet with God. Work hard, play passionately,
and rest completely.

A few weeks ago our pastor commented, "At

the end of my life, I don't want to look back and wonder what life would have been like if I had done it God's way." I trust this book has influenced your thinking so that at the end of your life you will look back and smile with satisfaction, knowing you made good choices. You did what you believed pleased God. Follow the plan suggested in this book:

1. Establish your lifelong priorities.

2. Confirm your season in life.

3. Set priorities for your yearly goals.

4. Decide which quarter you will work on each of those yearly goals.

5. Set weekly goals that accommodate the quarterly goals.

6. Create or organize a daily agenda.

After you complete that list, you will daily experience gratification, knowing that you are on target for accomplishing what you want to do over your entire lifetime.

Quoting again from Helmut Thielicke,

Only one thing is needful and that is
this hand of the Father, which is Jesus
Christ himself. When we hold on to that
hand we have everything — life and
salvation, peace and freedom from care;
and then quite incidentally, "in sleep,"
as that wonderful phrase of Scripture
puts it (Ps. 127:2), we are also given
what this hand has to give: the pennies
and crumbs, the food and drink, shoes
and clothing, and everything that we
need for life.

Sometimes it's difficult to understand the motives
behind our goals. As Christian women our desire
must be to please God; yet we have personal
preferences as human beings. Are these preferences mutually exclusive? Is it acceptable to
choose what I, as a woman, prefer doing?

The key is *focus*. Where is your focus? Is it on
pleasing God or yourself? Saturate yourself with
God and then allow Him to cultivate your
individual creativity and to give you the desires of
your heart.

I believe that if your focus is on God and you
ask Him to help you set your priorities and goals,
He gives you freedom in deciding how to accom-

plish them. He lets you fill in the details and methods to accomplish the goals yourself.

I don't believe God cares what style of furniture you have, as long as you don't become preoccupied with furniture rather than with Him. I don't believe you need to ask His permission to turn off the light switch or about which grocery store to patronize. I believe He cares more about who you *are*, how you love Him, and how you extend His love to the world, than He does about what details you plan in executing that focus.

If your focus is on Him, I believe you can relax and count on Him to change your direction if He has something specifically in mind for you to do other than what you're currently planning. Solomon tells us in the Proverbs to make plans, counting on God to direct us.

Have you gone to the tower even as Habakkuk went to search for God's perspective? I trust you traveled there and sought God's wisdom on a plan for your life. That is the first and most critical step toward securing a significant future.

By using the principles of this book, I hope you will say yes to that "best" plan and no to other "good" things which would distract you from following that blueprint. I trust you will have courage to say no to things which would keep you from experiencing the life Jesus talked about when He said, "I have come that you may have life, and have it to the full" (John 10:10).

My prayer for you is that you live life to the full, that you experience God's incredible love for you, that you will smile with pleasure knowing that the choices you make please God — and please you too.

The principle of this book is simple: Go before God and focus on Him and who He is. Ask Him to help you decide what He would have you do with your life that will ultimately please Him and bring about your end purpose of becoming more like His Son, Jesus Christ. Take time to listen carefully, and when He burdens your heart with objectives, break those down into workable units; then execute those units...one step at a time.

I'd like to end with a prayer taken from an old book of Pilgrim's prayers.

> Lord, I have time;
> I have plenty of time,
> all the time you give me,
> the years of my life,
> the days of my years,

the hours of my days,
they are all mine.
Mine to fill, quietly, calmly,
but to fill completely, up to the brim,
to offer them back to you...
I am not asking you, Lord,
for time to do this and then that,
but for your grace to do conscientiously,
in the time that you give me,
what you enable me to do...
what *you* want me to do.

For further information about Cheryl's speaking schedule
or about the Day-Focus system, write to:

Cheryl Biehl
Post Office Box 6128
Laguna Niguel, California 92677

telephone: 714-495-8850